THE MISSING PIECE

What Great Teams Do That Others Overlook

By Patrick Veroneau, MS

Published by Maison Vero
3002 Dow Avenue,
Suite 112 Tustin, CA 92780

Maison Vero is a professional publishing house that partners with rising authors to bring their thought leadership to the world. By respecting the copyright of an author's intellectual property, you enable Maison Vero and the author to continue publishing exceptional books for years to come. We thank you for supporting the author's copyright by purchasing an authorized edition of this book.

Inquiries may be directed to: Maison Vero, 3002 Dow Avenue, Suite 112 Tustin, CA 92780, or info@graymilleragency.com.

For information about special discounts for bulk purchases, please call 1-949-333-4872 or email info@graymilleragency.com.

Maison Vero is a partner brand of The Gray + Miller Agency a speaking, literary, and talent consortium.

For more information on the talent represented by The Gray + Miller Agency, or to bring any of our thought leaders to your organization or live event please visit our website at graymilleragency.com

Cover Design: Zach Sharples
Book Design: Mel Wise

Manufactured in the United States of America

Paperback 978-1-969508-04-2   E-book.   978-1-969508-09-7
Hardcover 978-1-969508-05-9

PRAISE FOR *THE MISSING PIECE*

"*The Missing Piece* is a compelling, actionable guide for anyone looking to build and lead truly cohesive, high-trust, high-performing teams. Backed by research and brought to life with practical insight, Veroneau equips leaders to build the kind of team culture where people collaborate, contribute, and thrive. It's a timely and actionable guide for anyone committed to unleashing the greatness in their team."

—Stephen M. R. Covey, *The New York Times* and #1 *Wall Street Journal* bestselling author of *The Speed of Trust* and *Trust & Inspire*

"*The Missing Piece* has the ability to push any team that wants to be great. While there are numerous guiding principles, if you are a business, family, sports team, or an organization, his clarity and articulation of Support, Celebrate, and Challenge provides the basic prescription for sustained performance and success if you follow them daily."

—Jude Killy, NCAA Division 1 Director of Athletics, University of Maine

"I absolutely love this book!!! It is truly a playbook that, if followed, will grow teams, turn teams around and strengthen an already winning team."

–Christi Green, Chief Human Resource Officer, Sanal NAPA Auto Parts

"This book explains what I've lived as a nurse and a leader, authentic recognition doesn't just lift spirits, it changes the brain. That insight has shaped how I show up for my team."

—Kim Force, DNP, RNC-MNN, Senior Director of Nursing

"*The Missing Piece* is the owner's manual for the most important piece of equipment in any organization: it's people. No leader can afford not to read this."

—Myles Morneault PT, DPT, OCS Director of Rehab Services

CONTENTS

Foreword by Jim Huling..ix

Introduction: Don't Hope For A Great Team—Build One...........1

PART ONE:
UNDERSTANDING THE FOUNDATION OF A GREAT TEAM

Chapter 1: Great Teams and One Percent.................................13
Why So Many Teams Struggle and What Science Tells Us About Success

Chapter 2: The Power of a "Believe" System.............................27
Building the Mindset That Makes Everything Possible

Chapter 3: The NEEDS Model: A Foundation for Stronger
Teams, Families, and Relationships...37
Understanding What Drives Human Engagement

Chapter 4: Building the Bridges That Carry
Teams to Success...53
The CABLES Model for Unshakeable Trust

PART TWO: BECOMING A GREAT TEAMMATE

Chapter 5: Great Teams Can Only Exist
With Great Teammates..79
Supporting, Celebrating, and Challenging Yourself

Chapter 6: Great Teams and One Percent.................................93
A Framework for Turning Goals Into Results

PART THREE: BECOMING A GREAT TEAM

Chapter 7: Why Support Comes First 111

Creating Psychological Trust and Trust

Chapter 8: Why Celebration Matters 129

Fueling Motivation and Reinforcing Excellence

Chapter 9: Why Challenge Comes Last 143

Moving From Accountability to Ownership

Chapter 10: Turning Insight Into Action:
Ownership Uncovered 165

Implementation Strategies for Lasting Change

Work Cited 179

About the Author 183

DOWNLOADS

Appendix A: How Great Is My Team? Assessment Tool
Appendix B: CABLES Relationship-Bridge Assessment
Appendix C: NEEDS Model Quick-Reference Guide
Appendix D: The POWER Journal for Well-Being

FOREWORD

There's a moment I've experienced in almost every coaching engagement, whether I'm working with a newly promoted leader, a seasoned CEO, or a team navigating high-stakes change. The moment looks different on the surface, but the theme underneath is always the same:

They've mastered their role.
But their team isn't where it needs to be.

They've worked hard. Built relationships. Delivered results. But somehow, the team still feels... disconnected. Unaligned. Not broken but not thriving. Not toxic but not energized.

And that's when the conversation shifts from individual performance to shared culture. From what the leader is doing to what the team is becoming.

That's where this book begins.
And it's why I believe so deeply in it.

Patrick Veroneau has written something rare—a book that doesn't just tell you what a great team looks like, it teaches you how to build one. It's part field guide, part invitation, and part mirror showing you what's working, what's missing, and what's possible when you choose to lead differently.

I first came to know Patrick through his speaking and writing; but over time, I've had the privilege of seeing something even more important: his heart. This book isn't a collection of leadership theories. It's a reflection of the kind of leader Patrick has chosen to be—one grounded in research, yes, but even more in integrity, humility, and real-world experience. His insights are battle-tested. His frameworks are field-ready. And his vision is one we need now more than ever.

Patrick's earlier book *The Leadership Bridge* focused on strengthening one-to-one relationships. *The Missing Piece* builds on that foundation and elevates it. Because strong leaders matter. But strong teams? That's where the real magic happens. That's where the values you stand for show up not just in your words but in your culture.

As someone who's spent the last two decades coaching over two hundred senior executives in five countries and who's had the honor of coauthoring *The 4 Disciplines of Execution*, I've seen what makes the difference in the long run. It's not just vision. Or strategy. Or even execution. It's *the space between people*—how they communicate, how they trust, how they challenge each other, and how they stay connected when things get hard.

That's what Patrick illuminates with such clarity in this book.

Let me pause to name three of the many takeaways that stood out for me and that I believe will stay with you long after the final chapter:

1. Extraordinary teams aren't explained. They're engineered.

Patrick teaches us that team culture isn't something we inherit, it's something we architect, one small behavior at a time. And what separates great teams isn't just their output, it's their design. From his CABLES model to the three-pillar framework of Support, Celebrate, and Challenge, Patrick gives you a blueprint that's both powerful and practical. You don't have to guess what matters most. You just have to build it with intention.

2. Support and celebration earn the right to challenge.

One of the most powerful shifts I've seen in executive teams happens when challenge no longer feels like a threat but an act of commitment. Patrick explains with clarity and heart why leaders who rush to challenge without first establishing trust and recognition often find themselves pushing against resistance instead of pulling toward growth. But when your team feels supported and seen when effort is celebrated and connection is real, challenge becomes a catalyst. It's not what breaks the team. It's what makes the team.

3. The one percent shift is real and it changes everything.

One of the most memorable parts of this book is Patrick's reminder that teams rarely succeed or fail in a single moment. Culture is built in increments. In the check-in you almost skipped. In the idea you chose to affirm. In the frustration you decided to pause and explore instead of brushing it aside. The difference between a functional team and a great one often lies in what happens when no one's watching and in the daily habits that either deepen trust or slowly unravel it.

Let me offer one story from my coaching work.

I was working with a CEO whose team had stalled, not in performance, but in energy. The numbers looked fine, but the culture had flatlined. There was no sense of joy. No fire. Just competence, drifting toward compliance. At our first offsite, I asked each executive to write down one thing they were grateful for from a teammate—something they had noticed but never said.

It was a small exercise. Quiet. But it changed everything.

One by one, leaders began reading what they had written. Gratitude turned into connection. Connection turned into vulnerability. And what emerged was a space where challenge could finally be heard, because people knew they were seen. That team didn't need more drive. They needed more humanity.

That's the wisdom this book holds.

Because The Missing Piece isn't about tactics, it's about transformation. Not the kind that comes from a keynote or a single insight, but the kind that happens when leaders choose to lead from the inside out. When we stop hoping for alignment and start building it one conversation, one behavior, one moment at a time.

Patrick reminds us that culture is not created by slogans on a wall. It's created by what your team does when things get hard. And this book equips you with the tools to shape those moments wisely, intentionally, and with love.

So take your time with this book. Don't just read it, live with it. Bring it to your team. Reflect on the examples. Try the prompts. Ask the hard questions. And then begin to build, layer by layer, the culture your people are quietly longing for.

Great teams are not accidents.

They are not the product of luck or charisma.

They are forged by leaders who care deeply, think clearly, and act consistently.

You'll find all three in these pages. And you'll find them in Patrick.

I'm honored to endorse this book and the man who wrote it. The world needs more teams like the ones described here. And it needs more leaders willing to do the work to build them.

If you're holding this book, I believe you're one of them. Let's get to work.

—**Jim Huling**, coauthor of The Wall Street Journal bestseller The 4 Disciplines of Execution and executive coach to CEOs in five countries

INTRODUCTION
DON'T HOPE FOR A GREAT TEAM— BUILD ONE

Something isn't working.

You feel it every day. The meeting where good ideas go to die. The talented person who's stopped speaking up. The team that has everything it needs to win but can't seem to pull together. The strategy that looks brilliant on paper but stalls in execution.

You've tried to fix it. More accountability. Better communication tools. Clearer goals. Team-building exercises. And yet, the gap between what your team is capable of and what it's actually achieving keeps widening.

Here's what too many seem to be misunderstanding when it comes to solving their team's or organization's current problems: The solution does not reside in a new accountability system or initiative to drive performance. And the cost of that mistake is compounding daily.

The Crisis That's Accelerating

There are some concerning trends happening right now across every industry and context. While there has been an increased focus over the last five years on accountability systems to improve behaviors and performance, there has been a significant erosion of employee engagement during that same period. That is not a coincidence.

Gallup's 2024 research reveals that employee engagement has hit a ten-year low. Only thirty-one percent of employees are engaged at work. Management engagement has dropped to twenty-seven percent, the lowest ever recorded.

This isn't just about motivation or morale. It's about fundamental structure. Culture Partners' comprehensive Workplace Accountability

Study of over forty thousand employees reveals exactly why traditional accountability approaches keep failing:

- Eighty-five percent of employees aren't even sure what their organization is trying to achieve.
- Ninety-three percent are unable to align their work or take accountability for desired results.
- Eighty-two percent of managers either try to hold others accountable but fail, or avoid it altogether.
- Eighty percent say feedback only happens when things go wrong or doesn't happen at all.

Think about those numbers. Despite decades of leadership development, despite millions spent on accountability systems and performance management, nine out of ten people can't align their work with organizational goals. Eight out of ten leaders can't effectively hold people accountable.

This isn't just a workplace problem. Athletic teams with championship talent are underperforming. Families with every advantage feel disconnected. Relationships that should thrive are barely surviving.

The pattern is universal and accelerating: We've been solving the wrong problem. And every day we continue down this path, the situation compounds in the wrong direction.

Why Our Focus on More Accountability Keeps Failing

The word "accountability" comes from the Latin *accomptare*, meaning "to account, render account, to reckon," and the Old French *aconter*, "to count." At its core, accountability is transactional. External. It asks: Did you do what you were supposed to do? Can you account for your actions?

That's why it creates compliance but not commitment. Reporting but not ownership. Checking boxes but not caring deeply.

When I ask individuals in my workshops who would look forward to a reckoning for their performance, I have yet to have anyone raise their hand.

Culture Partners CEO Roger Connors, who led the study, stated it directly: "There's a crisis of accountability in organizations today, a crisis of epidemic proportions." The research confirms that accountability is perceived as strictly consequential and almost entirely after the fact."

People experience it as something negative that happens to them, not as something that empowers them.

Now consider the word "ownership." It derives from Old English *āgen*, meaning "one's own, belonging to oneself." Ownership is internal. It's the difference between "I have to" and "I want to because this matters to me."

That difference isn't semantic. It's the gap between teams that are average or struggle and teams that are great.

Here's what makes this urgent: Ownership cannot be demanded, mandated, or measured into existence. It emerges only when you build the right structure in the right sequence with the right materials. And right now, with ninety-three percent of people unable to take accountability for results, most teams have overlooked this missing piece: ownership.

Ownership cannot be demanded, mandated, or measured into existence.

Let me show you what that master blueprint looks like.

The Structure That Changes Everything

Recently I visited the Queensferry Crossing in Scotland. It is the bridge I often use as the analogy to describe how great teams are built.

This bridge stretches 1.7 miles across the Firth of Forth: three massive towers rising from the water, connected by thousands of steel cables. Each tower is structurally impressive, capable of carrying tremendous weight independently.

But here's what matters: Without the precise connections between those towers, you'd have three isolated structures standing in the water. Potential without function. Strength without purpose. The bridge couldn't serve anyone because the pieces, however well built, weren't properly integrated.

Look at your team right now. You likely have talented people. You might have solid relationships. You probably have clear goals. But if ownership isn't emerging, if engagement is declining, if results aren't matching potential, you're probably missing the connections.

And without those connections, everything remains incomplete, no matter how hard people work. As I watched hundreds of passengers cross the bridge, I'm guessing none of them thought about the soil tests that found bedrock necessary to build the towers, the materials science that selected each cable, the construction sequencing that built each tower in the right order, or the maintenance protocols that were established to prevent its structural decline.

In the following chapters, you are going to become the architect, engineer, and builder of an even more impressive structure: a great team.

You are going to learn to create an environment so well structured that excellence becomes natural, where the right behaviors emerge not through force but through design.

Why This Book Exists

This is not another collection of leadership theories or inspiring anecdotes. This is a master blueprint based on how great teams are actually built to last.

Early in publishing, my editor observed: "Patrick, you have quite a few different models in this book."

They were right, and here's why that's essential rather than excessive.

This is a master blueprint based on how great teams are actually built to last. When structural engineers design a bridge, they don't use one simple formula. They integrate soil mechanics, materials science, load calculations, environmental factors, construction sequencing, and maintenance protocols. Each discipline is distinct. Each is nonnegotiable. You cannot build a bridge that lasts by choosing only the convenient parts of the engineering.

The same principle applies to building great teams.

If I gave you only one model (say, "Support, Celebrate, Challenge"), you'd know WHAT to do but not HOW to do it (that's where CABLES comes in), or WHY people respond the way they do (that's where NEEDS comes in), or WHETHER you have the personal foundation to sustain it (that's where Chapter 5 comes in).

This book isn't complicated. It's comprehensive. That comprehensiveness is what transforms good intentions into sustainable results.

You've tried partial solutions. The declining engagement numbers and the stark findings from organizations like the Culture Partners survey prove those approaches aren't working. It's time for the complete system.

What This Master Blueprint Delivers

Chapter 1: The One Percent Principle = Understanding Load Stress

How teams fail through small daily declines that seem insignificant until the structure collapses. This is your diagnostic.

Chapter 2: Believe System = Soil Testing and Bedrock

If people don't believe change is possible or worth the effort, you're building on marsh. Everything you construct will sink. This establishes your foundation.

Chapter 3: NEEDS = Building Materials (Foundation Supports)

Understanding the five core needs that drive all human engagement, motivation, and performance.

Chapter 4: CABLES = Building Materials (Steel Cables)

Six specific behaviors that build relationships strong enough to carry weight under pressure.

Chapter 5: Great Teammates = Personnel and Training

You cannot give what you don't have. This chapter ensures you're personally ready to lead the build.

Chapter 6: SET Goals = Construction Project Management

How to execute long-term builds without the momentum loss that kills most change initiatives.

Chapter 7: Support (First Tower) = Detailed Engineering-Blueprint 1

Building psychological trust that holds under pressure. Exactly which behaviors, in which sequence.

Chapter 8: Celebrate (Second Tower) = Detailed Engineering-Blueprint 2

Building sustainable motivation and momentum. Exactly which behaviors, in which sequence.

Chapter 9: Challenge (Central Tower) = Detailed Engineering-Blueprint 3

Building the ownership that transforms accountability into commitment. This is where the missing piece is revealed.

Chapter 10: Implementation = Maintenance Schedule

How to preserve what you've built and prevent the one percent decline that erodes structures over time.

Every framework is research-backed and field-tested across business teams, athletic programs, families, and relationships. You'll see how to apply it whether your team works in person, remotely, or in hybrid arrangements.

The Visual Guide to Your Journey

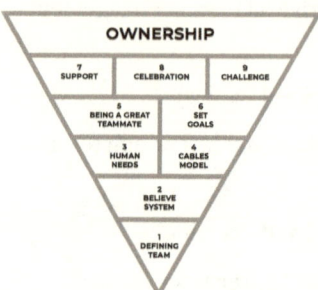

At the beginning of each chapter, you'll see an inverted pyramid balanced on its point. This represents ownership—the missing piece we're working toward. Once built, it becomes the broad foundation that holds everything else together. Without ownership, teams remain average or struggle.

As you progress through this book, you'll see this visual fill in one section at a time. The early chapters form the narrow point. From there, we build the three essential towers: Support, Celebrate, and Challenge. Only when all three are properly connected does ownership emerge. What appeared unstable becomes unshakeable as the completed missing piece is revealed and put in place.

This is a powerful analogy that great teams are not unlocked in a single step. They are built piece by piece until ownership finally puts everything into place.

What This Requires From You

Let me be direct: This book requires commitment, not just interest. Not just reading but implementing. Not just understanding but building.

The hardest work comes in the construction phase. But once the bridge is properly built, maintenance requires far less energy than you're currently spending trying to hold a broken structure together through sheer force of will.

Unfortunately, the majority of people who read leadership and teambuilding books, while they can cite the concepts and speak the language, often fail to apply or model the concepts consistently and continuously long enough to have a positive impact on their teams. As a result, teams often end up worse off than they were before.

But you're reading this because you recognize that partial solutions create partial results. Because you understand that your team is capable of more. Because ninety-three percent of people being unable to align their work with results isn't acceptable when the blueprint for sustainable excellence exists.

The question isn't whether this approach works. Thousands of teams across every context demonstrate that it does.

The question is whether you'll commit to building the complete structure, or whether you'll attempt another shortcut that keeps you where you are.

The Path Forward

The declining engagement isn't random. It's the predictable outcome of building the wrong structure. When eighty-five percent of employees don't know what their organization is trying to achieve, when eighty-two percent of employees suggest they fail at or avoid holding others accountable, when feedback only happens when things go wrong, we've been measuring the wrong thing, building the wrong foundation, focusing on compliance when we need ownership.

Ownership cannot be counted or reported. It can only be developed when individuals understand why people engage, how relationships strengthen, and what sequence creates sustainable results. But this will only happen if you believe it is worth the effort it will take to build a great team.

You now have a choice. You can continue with the partial solutions that create temporary improvements and inevitable decline, or you can commit to building the complete structure that transforms how your team operates.

The master blueprint is in your hands. The materials are identified. The sequence is clear.

Great teams aren't born. They're built. Intentionally. Systematically. With precision.

HOW TO READ THIS BOOK:
Your Construction Guide

Before you begin Chapter 1, understand how to navigate this blueprint effectively. This orientation ensures you can execute the build successfully.

THE INTEGRATED SYSTEM

You'll encounter several frameworks in this book:

- **The NEEDS Model** explains WHY people engage or withdraw.
- **The CABLES Behaviors** show HOW to build relationships that carry weight.
- **Support, Celebrate, Challenge** reveals WHAT great teams do in sequence.
- **SET Goals** provides project management for long-term execution.
- **The CATCH Model** gives you the conversation framework for constructive challenge.

These aren't competing initiatives. They're integrated components of one complete system. Bridge engineers don't choose between soil mechanics OR materials science OR load calculations. They use all of them, because structural integrity requires it.

Your team's excellence requires the same comprehensive approach.

THREE IMPLEMENTATION PATHS

PATH 1: THE RAPID-IMPLEMENTATION TRACK

Week 1: Download the "How Great Is My Team Assessment."
Read Introduction and Chapter 1 thoroughly.

Master the One Percent Principle and understand what's at stake.

Week 2: Skim Chapters 2 through 6 for awareness.

Understand that these elements exist and why they matter. Don't try to master them yet.

Weeks 3 to 4: Deep-read Chapters 7 through 9.

Support, Celebrate, Challenge. Focus your initial implementation here.

Weeks 5 to 6: Reference foundation chapters as gaps emerge.

As you implement, you'll discover which foundation elements need strengthening.

Within 90 Days: Complete second full read.

Foundation chapters make more sense after you've begun building.

Why This Works: Creates immediate visible progress while building comprehensive understanding over time.

PATH 2: THE COMPLETE BLUEPRINT (RECOMMENDED)

First Read: Download the "How Great Is My Team Assessment." Read all 10 chapters to understand how everything integrates.

Second Read: Use assessment tools to identify your weakest areas.

Third Read: Deep-dive on specific components requiring strengthening.

Time Investment: 8 to 10 hours over 2 to 3 weeks.

Why This Works: You'll see the complete system before making construction decisions.

PATH 3: THE DIAGNOSTIC APPROACH

Step 1: Download the "How Great Is My Team Assessment." Read Introduction and Chapter 1.

Step 2: Complete assessment tools in Appendices A and B.

Step 3: Read chapters addressing your biggest gaps first.

Step 4: Fill in remaining chapters for complete system understanding.

Maximizing Each Chapter

Every chapter includes:

Core Content: Research, frameworks, application across contexts.

Key Takeaways: Essential insights requiring retention.

Reflection Questions: Diagnostic tools for honest assessment.

Practice Prompts: Immediate actions before progressing.

Bridge Connections: Integration with other components.

Use every element. Reflection questions are diagnostic tools, not optional exercises. Practice prompts are the beginning of implementation, not suggestions.

Your Commitment

Before turning to Chapter 1, commit to this:

I will read this book with the intent to build, not just to understand.

Understanding is necessary but insufficient. Great teams are built by people who transform insight into action—who implement, adjust, and persist.

The blueprint is in your hands. The construction begins now.

Let's get to work.

PART ONE

UNDERSTANDING
THE FOUNDATION
OF A GREAT TEAM

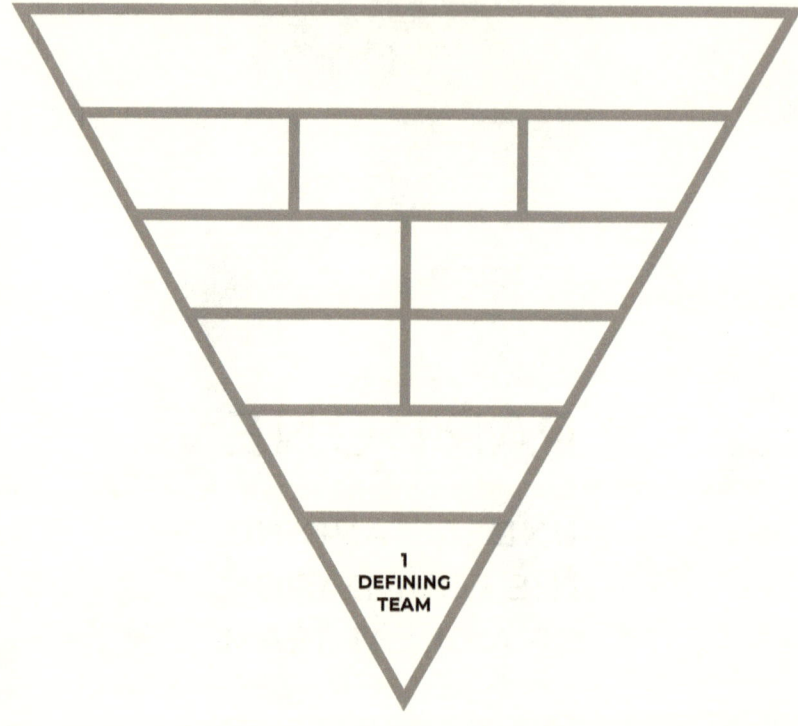

CHAPTER 1
GREAT TEAMS AND ONE PERCENT

"Alone we can do so little; together we can do so much."

– HELEN KELLER

Every day, your team is getting one percent better or one percent worse. You probably don't notice it happening: a missed check-in here, an unacknowledged contribution there, a difficult conversation avoided. But by year's end, that invisible drift compounds into either a ninety-seven percent decline or a 3,700 percent improvement. Many leaders never realize which direction they're heading until their best people walk out the door.

That's the one percent drift, and it's happening in your team right now.

THE MATH THAT CHANGES EVERYTHING

Improve one percent daily for 70 days, and you're nearly twice as strong. Decline one percent daily, and you're half as effective. The problem? Neither change feels urgent day to day. That's the trap that catches most leaders off guard. While all teams will experience struggles or one percent declines at times, the great teams overshadow these declines with many more one percent positive-growth days.

A manager I coached several years ago moved his office to another floor during a reorganization. It was just one floor and, technically, only few extra steps away from his team. Yet, within six months, two key people left and others felt disconnected. It wasn't intentional neglect on his part, just the compound effect of small, missed moments of connection. To rebuild, he implemented regular check-ins and casual drop-ins. After several months of consistent presence, the team's morale improved dramatically. During one of our coaching sessions, he reflected that he had completely underestimated the power of small, consistent actions such as greeting people in the morning, checking in with them during the day, or asking them how their weekends went and being interested in their responses.

Success and failure both happen in increments. Whether it's an athletic team, an organization, a family, or a personal relationship, what we do consistently becomes the culture we create. The daily choices that seem insignificant in the moment become the defining characteristics of our teams over time.

This principle applies universally because human behavior operates on patterns. When we consistently model supportive behavior, people learn to trust. When we regularly celebrate progress, people stay motivated. However, when we habitually avoid difficult conversations, people learn that accountability is optional. The one percent drift doesn't discriminate; it compounds whatever we feed it. While as individuals and as teams we are always going to experience bad days or have an unnoticed one percent negative shift, the importance is in which way we are trending.

WHERE THE ONE PERCENT DRIFT SHOWS UP

The pattern is universal, but it manifests differently across contexts. Understanding where to look for the drift helps leaders catch it before it becomes irreversible.

Business: When Talent Hits a Trust Ceiling

A business team can have all the right talent and resources but still underperform if trust is weak. Employees hesitate to speak up in meetings, worried about how they'll be perceived. Collaboration becomes transactional, with team members focusing on their own tasks instead of working toward shared goals. Decision making slows because no one feels confident taking ownership.

At first, these issues don't seem like a crisis, just normal organizational life. But over time, they quietly shift the culture. Deadlines start getting missed, employees disengage, and communication becomes surface level. Eventually, the best people either leave or stop trying, and leadership wonders what went wrong.

This experience connects directly to what researchers call psychological trust, a concept that's been explored since the 1970s but has become increasingly recognized as foundational to team performance. When people don't feel safe to take risks, share ideas, or admit mistakes, even the most talented teams struggle to reach their potential.

The erosion happens through seemingly minor behaviors: gossiping about team members, not taking responsibility for mistakes, blaming others, taking sole credit for successes, and withholding information that could help the team. Each instance might seem small; but collectively, they create an environment where trust becomes scarce and collaboration suffers.

While the phrase "trust is earned" sounds compelling, I've learned that strategically extending trust often motivates people to live up to that confidence. Yes, this approach occasionally backfires, but the upside of starting with trust far outweighs the occasional disappointment. When I present this to leaders, I often call it a "cost of doing business." I go on to explain that while some might take advantage of me and the situation, it is rare and has far more upside than down. This approach builds stronger relationships, greater commitment, and a foundation for genuine leadership.

The Hybrid Challenge: When Distance Amplifies Drift

The one percent drift becomes even more critical in hybrid and remote environments. When Sarah's camera is always off during meetings, it feels like a small thing. When Tom consistently joins calls a few minutes late, it seems minor. But these small digital disconnections compound faster than in-person oversights. A missed smile, a casual conversation that doesn't happen, a moment of recognition that gets lost in a muted microphone—these add up to cultural erosion at an accelerated pace.

What happens naturally in traditional office environments must be deliberately created in virtual settings. The "water cooler" factor that builds relationships disappears when we're all working from separate spaces. Without intentional effort, teams drift apart faster because the invisible threads that hold groups together—shared coffee conversations, quick check-ins between meetings, nonverbal cues that signal engagement—simply don't exist in digital environments.

Remote teams that thrive understand this amplified drift effect. They create systematic touchpoints for connection. They're more intentional about recognition because good work becomes less visible when people aren't physically present. They adapt their leadership behaviors to account for the reality that small disconnections have bigger consequences when physical proximity can't compensate.

The math remains the same, one percent better or worse each day, but the timeline accelerates. What might take months to erode in a traditional office setting can happen in weeks when teams are distributed. This isn't an argument against flexible work; it's a call for more intentional team leadership when physical presence isn't available to smooth over the small gaps in connection.

Sports: Scoreboards Don't Lie About Chemistry

It's easy to assume that the most skilled teams will win, but talent alone doesn't create championship performance. Trust, appreciation, and shared ownership do. Teams with great individual players but no interest in each other consistently underperform against less talented teams that actually function as units.

The 2011 Miami Heat assembled a superteam that seemed destined for immediate dominance. LeBron James, Dwyane Wade, and Chris Bosh had combined for six All-NBA First Team selections in the previous season alone. Yet, their first season together was marked by visible dysfunction. Wade and James often seemed to be taking turns rather than playing together, with both accustomed to being the primary ball handler and struggling to figure out when to defer. Bosh found himself relegated to watching from the corners, uncertain of his role and visibly frustrated. The team developed a reputation for isolation basketball and finger-pointing after losses. Their struggles culminated in a stunning NBA Finals defeat to the Dallas Mavericks, where LeBron's passive fourth-quarter performances became symbolic of a team that had not yet learned how to lift each other up in critical moments. The talent was undeniable, but they played like three great individual players, not one great team.

This pattern of ego undermining talent was not new to the NBA. Even Scottie Pippen, who would become legendary for his selfless play, once refused to return to the court in the final 1.8 seconds of a 1994 playoff game simply because coach Phil Jackson had drawn up the last shot for Toni Kukoc instead of him. Pippen sat at the end of the bench while his teammates fought without him, prioritizing his bruised pride over his team's championship hopes. It was not until the following season, after a humbling summer of reflection, after Wade began deferring to LeBron as the primary playmaker, after Bosh embraced his role as the facilitator who made winning plays rather than demanding touches, and after all three committed to holding each other accountable rather than protecting their individual brands, that the Heat finally transformed into champions. The lesson, illustrated across generations, was clear. Greatness does not transfer automatically to team success. It requires the humility to serve something larger than yourself.

Another story that perfectly illustrates the missing piece came from Lou Holtz's second year coaching at the University of South Carolina. After two players were arrested for dealing drugs, Holtz called a team meeting. What troubled him most wasn't the arrests themselves, but that the players hadn't trusted him enough to bring their issues to him first. A sophomore stood up and said, "Coach, I trust you, but there are a lot of players here I don't trust." Holtz seized the moment, telling the team that winning required more than talent—it required trust, caring about one another, and putting the team above self. He had every player write down everything they'd done to violate their teammates' trust, placed the notes in a bag, and burned them in a field. "From this point forward," he told them, "we will not tolerate anyone putting themselves above the team." It became one of the greatest turnarounds in college football history, proving that talent may fill a roster, but trust and shared commitment create great teams.

Families: The Strongest Team You'll Ever Play On

Families function as teams, even when they don't see themselves that way. Parents and children work together to create environments where everyone can thrive. But just like in workplaces and sports teams, small breakdowns in communication, left unaddressed, lead to long-term disconnection.

A child who used to share everything suddenly gives one-word answers. A parent who once made time for conversations now assumes silence means everything's fine. These shifts are easy to dismiss initially ("Life is just busy right now"), but as weeks turn into months, distance replaces connection. By the time parents recognize the problem, the habit of open conversation may already be lost.

The research is sobering. Harvard studies show that families maintaining regular shared meals report significantly higher levels of emotional connection, yet surveys indicate that over sixty percent of households have family dinners fewer than three times a week. What begins as missed meals becomes missed moments of connection.

Dr. John Gottman's work highlights that it's not the big events, but the small, everyday interactions (what he calls "emotional bids") that keep relationships strong. When we respond to these bids with attention and care, we strengthen trust and connection. When we consistently miss them, relationships gradually weaken.

I experienced this growing up as the youngest of ten kids in a household where money was absent but love was abundant. Despite limited financial resources, I never felt poor because of the connection and belonging our family created. With that many personalities under one roof, there was inevitable chaos and conflict, but there was also something powerful: We knew we were in it together. My parents and older siblings modeled what it meant to have each other's backs. When one of us struggled, others stepped up. When someone succeeded, we celebrated together. That experience didn't just shape my childhood; it gave me a template for what great teams could look like.

With my own family (my wife, Cyndi and our three children, Noah, Grace, and Josh), that belief has deepened. Our family team has evolved over the years. When the kids were younger, family meals kept us connected. As sports schedules filled evenings, we adapted, finding new ways to maintain our bond. Today, with two kids away at college and our oldest already graduated, we maintain connection through regular check-ins and conversations. Cyndi and I see ourselves as captains and coaches of our family team, knowing our connection sets the tone for everyone else.

The family team is unique because it's the team you're hopefully on for life. Teammates at work or in sports come and go, but family remains. Like any great team, it requires effort, attention, and daily commitment to stay strong. When we stop tending to small conversations and everyday connections, we risk weakening the team that matters most.

Relationships: The 5:1 Ratio That Predicts Success

Couples are teams too, and the same patterns apply. It's not the big arguments that end most relationships; it's the small, missed chances to connect. A kind word unsaid, a small gesture overlooked, a moment of support missed: these create the one percent slide that compounds over time.

Dr. John Gottman's research reveals what he calls "The Magic Ratio": Successful relationships maintain at least five positive interactions for every negative one. It's not about avoiding conflict, but ensuring that moments of kindness, affection, and support far outweigh tension or criticism. When that ratio tips in the wrong direction, even slightly and consistently, relationships erode.

Gottman also identified four specific behaviors that predict relationship failure: criticism, contempt, defensiveness, and stonewalling. These aren't always loud or dramatic; often they creep in subtly. A dismissive glance. A sarcastic remark. A defensive response instead of an open one. Over time, these small behaviors build barriers instead of bridges.

A survey by the American Psychological Association suggests that sixty-seven percent of couples experiencing relationship distress cite "growing apart" rather than a singular conflict as the root cause. "Growing apart" means the gradual loss of daily connection, missed moments that slowly widen the gap.

I often reflect that no one stands at the altar thinking, "I can't wait for the day we don't get along or want to get divorced." It sounds absurd, yet that's exactly what happens; not through intention, but through small, unnoticed changes over time—the one percent drift that accumulates until the cost of inattention catches up.

Cyndi and I have learned that relationship maintenance happens in small moments. Something as routine as grocery shopping becomes an opportunity for connection: no phones, no distractions, just conversation about meals and plans that creates more time we'll share together. These aren't grand gestures, but they're intentional choices to stay present with each other.

For over twenty years, I've maintained a tradition of writing poems for Cyndi's birthdays, our anniversaries, and Mother's Day. They highlight memories and milestones from our additional year together. They're often corny and definitely wouldn't win any literary awards, but they've become something she treasures and collects. I've never missed one, and there have been times when sitting down to write felt difficult or inconvenient. But I keep the commitment because I understand that letting it slip once makes it easier to skip the next time. That's the subtle slide that feels small in the moment but isn't.

Successful couples don't just manage big issues well; they pay attention to small, daily interactions that build or break their bond. Like great teams, strong couples make showing up for each other a consistent practice.

THE PATTERN IS UNIVERSAL

Whether the team exists in a boardroom, on a field, in a home, or in a marriage, the struggles follow the same pattern:

1. **The first signs of decline are subtle:** they don't announce themselves as crises.
2. **Small declines quietly shape culture:** what you tolerate, you teach.
3. **By the time problems are obvious, repair costs more than prevention.**

The encouraging truth? Small improvements compound just as powerfully when they're deliberate and consistent. The same mathematical principle that can destroy teams can also elevate them to extraordinary performance.

THE SCIENCE: WHY ENVIRONMENT BEATS TALENT

Research consistently shows that environment plays a bigger role in success than individual ability. When the right conditions exist, people engage, persist through challenges, and commit to shared goals. When those conditions are missing, even the most skilled teams struggle.

Harvard researcher Amy Edmondson found that the highest-performing teams weren't necessarily the most talented but those where people felt safe speaking up, taking risks, and making mistakes. This psychological trust allows teams to adapt, innovate, and problem-solve effectively. Without it, people hesitate, keep ideas to themselves, and play it safe.

Neuroscientist Paul Zak discovered that high-performing teams produce more oxytocin, a neurochemical linked to trust and cooperation. Teams with strong trust demonstrated higher productivity, lower stress, and greater job satisfaction. Trust isn't just a nice idea; it's wired into our biology.

Carol Dweck's research on growth mindset and Angela Duckworth's work on grit show that resilience isn't about natural toughness. It's about believing that effort leads to progress. Teams that embrace learning and effort as part of the process recover from setbacks faster and adapt more effectively.

The implications are profound: Talent alone never guarantees success, but the right environment can unlock potential in ways that surprise everyone involved.

What Great Teams Do: The Support → Celebrate → Challenge Framework

After studying hundreds of high-performing teams across different contexts, I've discovered that great teams practice three behaviors consistently and in a specific sequence:

SUPPORT→"We've got each other's backs." Support creates psychological trust. It's not about coddling; it's about presence, clarity, and genuine care. People need to know you're with them, not just managing them. That kind of support (authentic, grounded, and visible) builds trust that teams can count on.

CELEBRATE→ "We appreciate each other." Recognition isn't a perk; it's fuel. Celebration communicates what matters: effort, progress, courage, learning. When people feel genuinely appreciated and valued, they invest more deeply in the team's success.

CHALLENGE→ "We push each other." When challenge is delivered well, it's honest, direct, and specific. But it only works effectively when Support and Celebration are already established. Without that foundation, Challenge feels like criticism or attack.

THE SEQUENCE IS CRUCIAL

Support builds the foundation of trust. Celebrate raises morale. Only then can Challenge be received as invitation rather than criticism. Skip the foundation, and Challenge feels like an attack. Without Celebrate, Support feels hollow. Get the sequence right, and something powerful emerges: People don't just do what they're supposed to do; they take *ownership* of outcomes because they genuinely care.

HOW THIS WORKS IN PRACTICE

I once worked with a healthcare executive who had inherited a team through a hospital merger. The group had been poorly managed and lacked structure. From the start, he felt frustrated by their performance and, honestly, didn't trust them. That resentment showed up in his behavior, and the team responded with distrust and dislike. The divide grew wider each week.

After several coaching conversations, he acknowledged that he might have treated them unfairly. When I asked what he could do differently, he made a bold decision: He called a meeting and apologized. He admitted his missteps, expressed a sincere desire to build better relationships, and asked for their help. More importantly, he committed through both words and actions to having their backs moving forward.

The team saw something authentic: a leader modeling vulnerability, owning his behavior, and inviting partnership. Over time, they began showing up differently because he had demonstrated what support really looks like.

I learned this principle early in my career at Automatic Data Processing. It was my first role as a sales representative, working for a company that continuously supported its sales representatives through training and coaching. My regional sales manager, Bob Whittemore, was larger than life to me at that time. He was a leader who commanded both attention and respect. But more importantly, he was known for how generously he supported and celebrated those who worked for him. So when he pulled me aside during one of his visits to discuss my declining numbers, I didn't brace for attack. I leaned in.

He didn't threaten or reprimand me. Instead, he told me plainly that my current effort and results reflected less than what I was capable of achieving. That was it. No pressure, no performance ultimatum. Just a clear, honest challenge from someone who had already earned my trust. I left his office with renewed ownership and determination to raise my standards.

When Teams Hit Their Stride:
The Missing Piece Revealed

Ownership is what separates great teams from average and struggling ones. It's the difference between doing something because you have to and doing it because you genuinely care. When people take ownership, standards rise; not because someone is watching, but because excellence matters to them personally. They seek feedback without being asked, help others without being told, and push beyond expectations, because they're proud of the work and committed to the mission.

> Ownership is what separates great teams from average and struggling ones.

Just like the Queensferry Crossing, once everything is properly integrated, teams can move in both directions: forward through growth and challenge, back through reflection and recognition. Ownership isn't about perfect execution or always winning; it's about connection and shared commitment. The integrity of great teams depends on that structure being reinforced consistently over time.

As I close this chapter on teams, I want to leave you with an analogy I often share with the groups I work with. I begin by showing a series of pictures chronicling the construction of the Queensferry Crossing. Stage by stage, the images reveal the massive investment of materials, equipment, and human effort required to bring the bridge to life. Every resource was frontloaded into building it. But once the bridge was complete, the cranes, machinery, and labor were no longer needed. From that point forward, the focus shifted to ongoing care—ensuring the bridge was maintained and did not fall into disrepair.

The same is true of building a great team. Most of the energy and resources are invested up front in establishing support, celebration, and challenge. Once those foundations are in place, it takes far fewer resources to sustain greatness—but it still requires intentional effort. Too many teams remain average, or even struggle, because they are unwilling to make that initial investment. That is why the next chapter is so critical: it introduces the next element that develops the missing piece.

Key Takeaways

- Teams don't deteriorate overnight; they drift apart through unnoticed one percent declines.
- Environment beats talent; talent needs trust to thrive.
- Support→Celebrate→Challenge: sequence creates compound effect.
- Small, daily behaviors become culture.
- The hybrid challenge amplifies drift—digital environments require more intentional leadership.
- The missing piece isn't talent or strategy; it's ownership, which emerges when the sequence is followed consistently.

Reflection Questions

- Think about your current teams at work, at home, or in your relationships. Where might you be overlooking small signs of disconnection?
- Are you spending enough time celebrating progress, not just outcomes? If not, what small shift could you make?
- Where in your team are you seeing accountability but not ownership? What might you change to help move the culture forward?
- In hybrid or remote settings, how are you being more intentional about connection and recognition?
- What direction is your one percent moving?

Practice Prompt

Before moving on, take one small step: Find one opportunity today to genuinely celebrate someone in your life. Look for effort, progress, or contribution, no matter how small. As you do, reflect on this: When you celebrate consistently, you build the relational capital that makes it safe to challenge and grow together. Watch how this small act builds the foundation for future support and challenge. That's the one percent improvement that compounds.

What's Next

The one percent drift is universal, but it's not inevitable. Some leaders and teams consistently compound in the positive direction. What separates them isn't talent, resources, or luck. It's a specific mindset that treats growth as both possible and worth the effort. That mindset (and how to develop it in yourself and others) is where we turn next.

In Chapter 2, I will discuss why a "believe" system is vital before any construction is started when building the team. The need to believe provides the bedrock foundation needed to build a great team.

The question isn't whether the One Percent Rule works. The question is: What direction will you choose for your next one percent?

BLUEPRINT COMPONENT:

SOIL TESTING AND SITE SELECTION

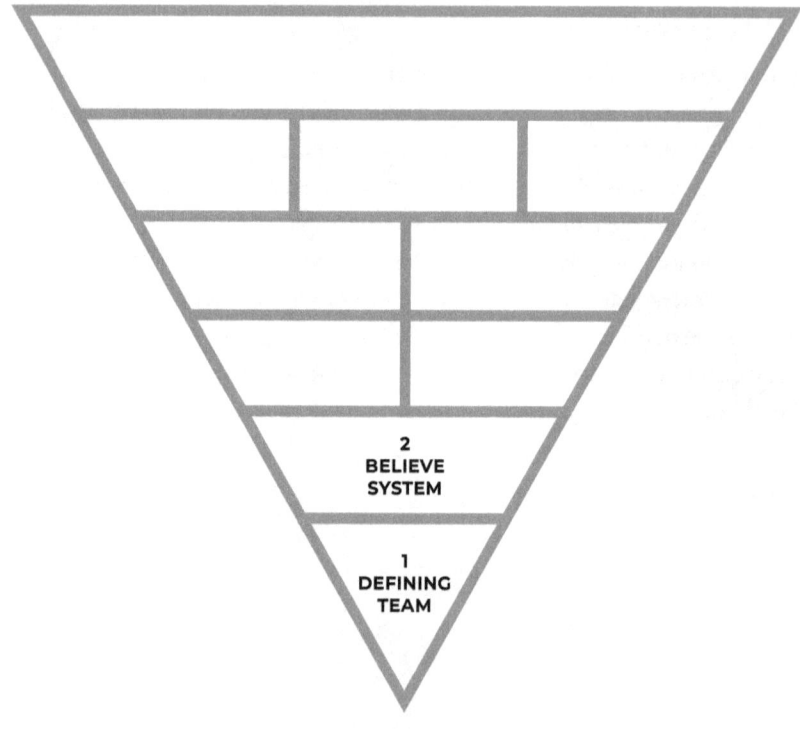

CHAPTER 2

THE POWER OF A "BELIEVE" SYSTEM

"Believe you can and you're halfway there."

– THEODORE ROOSEVELT

In the first session of every eight-week leadership series I run, I see a predictable pattern. Some participants come reluctantly: I call them the prisoners. Others are just happy to be out of their regular routine: the vacationers. And some arrive genuinely open to growth: the learners.

By the third session, a shift usually starts to occur. Someone who started skeptical approaches me something along the lines of, "I have to admit, I began as a prisoner, but this is actually helping me." The difference isn't in what I taught; it's in what they chose to believe about the importance of improving their leadership skills, the importance of building better teams, and their potential to grow.

That shift from resistance to openness, from compliance to conviction, is what separates teams that transform from those that just go through the motions. It's the difference between teams that create lasting change and those that create temporary compliance.

Why Most Development Programs Fail

Most team—and leadership—development initiatives often fail because they ask people to blindly adopt someone else's beliefs. Organizations try to impose belief systems from the outside: a set of values, principles, or expectations that teams are supposed to accept and follow. But great teams do something different. They develop their own "believe" systems.

Think about that one letter difference. Most organizations focus on *belief* systems: passive acceptance of handed-down principles. Great teams develop *believe* systems: active conviction that growth matters, is achievable, and worth the investment of time and energy to build.

Great teams develop
believe systems:
active conviction
that growth matters,
is achievable
and worth the
investment of time
and energy to build.

One is passive acceptance; the other is active conviction. One happens *to you*; the other happens *because of you*. Great teams don't just know what to do—they're convinced it's worth doing, and they're convinced they can do it.

Think of it like holding the master blueprint for a great team. You can study the design, understand how the pieces fit together, agree it's well-conceived, even discuss it intelligently with others, and that's *belief*. But *believe* is when you personally decide to invest the time, energy, and risk required to build it. It's when you commit to the hard conversations, the patient development, the uncomfortable growth moments. The blueprint doesn't change, but your relationship to it does. One keeps you nodding in agreement at the plan; the other puts you to work building something real. With *belief*, you acknowledge a great team can be built. With *believe*, you're convinced it's worth *your* investment to build it.

That shift is what this chapter is about. *Belief* is intellectual assent: agreeing that a principle makes sense or that a model is logical. But *believe* carries weight. It's personal. It's actionable. It means someone has crossed the line from passive agreement into willingness to commit.

It's the space between talking about leadership principles and actually applying them under pressure—in real-world relationships, when the stakes feel high and the margin for error feels small.

I've seen talented people stall out in their development, not because they lacked intelligence or insight, but because they never hit the "I believe" button.

The Neuroscience of Believing

Here's what happens in your brain when you make this transition: When you visualize yourself succeeding at something, your brain activates the same neural pathways triggered when you actually perform that task. You're not just imagining success, you're literally rehearsing it. This is why top athletes spend hours in mental preparation. They're not fantasizing; they're training their brains for peak performance.

Studies show that the way you speak to yourself directly impacts your stress levels, motivation, and performance outcomes. When you shift from "I can't do this" to "I'm learning how to do this," you're not just being optimistic. You're rewiring your brain for growth.

Some research suggests that people with growth mindsets actually produce different stress-hormone patterns when facing challenges. They see obstacles as opportunities, which creates a completely different physiological response than those who see obstacles as threats.

When you visualize yourself succeeding... You're not just imagining success, you're literally rehearsing it.

This isn't feel-good psychology. It's measurable neuroscience that explains why some leaders create lasting change while others create temporary compliance.

Success Happens Twice

Before any significant achievement can occur, it must first take root as a thought, a vision of what could be. This is where the power of visualization becomes crucial for building your believe system. Everything we have done or accomplished we have first seen in our mind.

Consider Kyle Carpenter, a U.S. Marine who, on November 21, 2010, saved the lives of his fellow Marines in Afghanistan by throwing himself on a grenade to shield them. His selfless act left him severely injured, losing his right eye, enduring multiple fractures to his right arm, and suffering numerous other life-threatening wounds.

In the face of these harrowing injuries, it would have been easy for Kyle to accept defeat. Instead, he chose to build a believe system around his potential for recovery. He refused to see himself as someone defined by his injuries and set his sights on a goal that seemed impossible: running the Marine Corps Marathon.

In his own words, he started small: "If I could sit up in bed, I could work on getting my feet off the edge of my bed. If I could hang my feet off the edge of my bed, I could stand. If I could stand, I could take a step. If I could take a step, I could walk. If I could walk, I could run, and if I could run, one day I could complete that marathon."

Kyle's story illustrates a fundamental principle: He saw success in his mind first, then created it in reality through systematic action.

Notice how this applies to teams. Before a team can function at its highest potential, it must first believe in its collective ability to succeed. Team members must see, in their mind's eye, the group operating at its best, supporting one another, celebrating wins, and challenging each other to reach greater heights. As well, they must believe it is worth the investment in time and effort required to develop a great team.

This process of visualization becomes essential when building a believe system. It's not enough to wish for greatness. You must mentally and emotionally commit to the idea of greatness. By visualizing success, you're telling your brain that this isn't just possible but already in motion.

Moreover, this process connects directly to a fundamental principle of the believe system: that you have the ability to shape your outcomes. When we visualize success, we reinforce our own agency in achieving it. The more vividly we imagine the successful execution of supporting, celebrating, and challenging each other, the more likely we are to take the necessary steps to make that vision reality.

Fixed vs. Growth: The Foundation

The foundation of any believe system rests on what psychologist Carol Dweck calls "mindset"—the underlying beliefs people have about learning and intelligence.

Fixed mindset assumes abilities and intelligence are static traits. People with this mindset believe that if they're not good at something immediately, they never will be. This leads to avoiding challenges, fearing failure, and giving up when things get difficult.

Growth mindset is grounded in the belief that abilities can be developed through effort, learning, and perseverance. People with a growth mindset see challenges as opportunities, view setbacks as lessons, and understand that effort leads to mastery.

Consider Michael Jordan, widely regarded as one of the greatest basketball players of all time. Jordan was famously cut from his high school varsity team as a sophomore. He came home devastated and cried with his mother, Deloris. Rather than letting him accept this as proof he wasn't good enough, she challenged him with simple but powerful advice: "If you really want it, you work hard over the summer." That summer, Jordan practiced relentlessly, the basketball rarely leaving his hand. He embodied the growth mindset (with the help of his mother) by turning failure into motivation rather than limitation, establishing a pattern that would define his entire career.

In the business world, Indra Nooyi's rise to CEO of PepsiCo demonstrates growth mindset in action. When she joined PepsiCo as a strategist, she didn't have beverage-industry experience. Instead of staying in her lane, she immersed herself in learning every aspect of the business, from supply chains to consumer trends. She transformed PepsiCo by challenging the status quo with her "Performance with Purpose" vision, even when it meant facing skepticism from the board and Wall Street. Nooyi saw the company's challenges not as fixed constraints but as opportunities to reimagine what a food-and-beverage company could become.

A Personal Investment in Mindset

This belief in the power of mindset isn't just something I teach. It's something I have challenged myself to live. Last Christmas, I made what might seem like an unusual choice: I gave each of my children a copy of Carol Dweck's *Mindset*. I genuinely believe it's the most important gift I've ever purchased for them.

Each is at a pivotal stage. Noah, our youngest, is a sophomore lacrosse player at Saint Michael's College in Vermont, navigating the challenges of competing at the Division II level. Grace, our middle child, is a senior at the University of Alabama, standing at the crossroads of choosing her career path. Josh, our oldest, is in a competitive sales position, facing the relentless pressures of a demanding market.

I told them all if they took the time to truly understand and model the principles in that book, it would be a game changer. Mindset is the great separator that can determine success or stagnation in every area of their lives.

Why share this personal decision? Because it is one of the most powerful endorsements I can provide on the vital importance of the need to develop a growth mindset if one is going to be part of a great team.

When everyone believes that improvement is possible, not just individually but collectively, it creates an environment of collaboration, problem solving, and resilience. With a growth mindset, teams become more open to feedback, more supportive of each other, and more willing to challenge one another in ways that drive collective progress.

Your Internal Search Engine

Your brain has a built-in search engine called the reticular activating system (RAS). This network of neurons filters the overwhelming amount of information you encounter every day, deciding what gets your attention and what stays in the background.

Here's what's crucial: This system is shaped by what you focus on. What you believe about yourself, your team, and your potential influences what your brain notices. When you adopt a believe system, you're effectively training your brain to tune in to opportunities, solutions, and people that align with your goals.

A simple example: When you start thinking about buying a particular car, suddenly you notice that model everywhere. Those cars were always there, but now your brain is tuned to them. The same thing happens with your goals and beliefs. When you focus on growth and progress, your brain highlights opportunities that support that focus.

This is essential when building a believe system. If you believe in your ability to build a great team—one that supports, celebrates, and challenges each other—your brain will start pointing out moments to do exactly that.

Changing Your Inner Dialogue

The most important conversation you have each day is the one you have with yourself. The late Wayne Dyer once pointed out that if people truly understood the impact of self-talk, they would be far more careful with their words. The way you speak to yourself shapes how you see the world, how you see yourself, and how you respond to challenges.

Positive self-talk helps you stay grounded when things are difficult. It reminds you that progress is possible and setbacks are part of the process. Negative self-talk feeds doubt and hesitation. It sounds like "I'm not good enough," "I'll never figure this out," or "Other people are just better than me."

The important thing to understand is that self-talk isn't automatic. It's something you can influence. Replace self-doubt with statements that focus on learning and progress. Instead of "I'm not good at this," try "I can get better at this with effort." Instead of "I'm not cut out for this," try "I'm building the skills I need to succeed."

Building Daily Practices

A believe system isn't a nice-to-have. It's a necessity for individuals and teams who want to thrive. Here's how to build an unshakeable believe system in your daily routine.

Start each morning by mentally rehearsing success. See yourself and your team operating at your best—supporting, celebrating, and challenging each other effectively. This isn't daydreaming. It's neural preparation for peak performance.

Throughout the day, notice the messages you give yourself. Are they building belief or feeding doubt? Make conscious shifts toward growth-oriented language. Train your brain to focus on possibilities rather than problems.

In the evening, intentionally notice moments that reinforce your belief in progress and potential. Write down one example each day. You're training your brain's search engine to find evidence that supports your goals.

When challenges arise, ask yourself: "Am I feeding my faith in what's possible or my fear of what might go wrong?" Choose faith consistently and watch how it transforms your approach to obstacles.

The Contagious Effect

When you commit to building a believe system, you're choosing to actively shape your reality. You're not waiting for success to happen, you're creating it. The work you put into cultivating this belief in yourself and your team transforms your mindset, shifts your behavior, and ultimately leads to greater performance.

What excites me even more is that believe systems are contagious. When team members see a leader who operates from conviction rather than compliance, they begin to shift their own mindset. When teammates support each other's growth instead of competing out of insecurity, the entire culture transforms.

Whether it's a Marine rebuilding his body, a director rebuilding her relationship with her team, or you rebuilding your approach to leadership, it always starts with a decision to believe growth is possible and worth the effort.

This choice becomes the foundation for everything else. In a world full of belief systems handed down from above, the courage to build your own believe system from within sets you apart. It's what transforms good intentions into lasting change, compliance into conviction, and groups of individuals into truly great teams.

Conviction is not a prerequisite for growth, but it is for greatness. You don't need every team member to start with full commitment. You just need enough momentum to help people move out of skepticism and into possibility. That's the power of great leadership. It's not about forcing conviction. It's about cultivating it.

Once you truly believe the work it takes to build a great team is worth it, the daily actions that create greatness become not just possible, they become inevitable.

Key Takeaways

- A believe system is active, built through intentional thought, self-talk, and action, not passive acceptance.
- Growth mindset helps you see challenges as opportunities for progress, not proof of inadequacy.
- Success happens twice: first in your mind through visualization, then in reality through action.
- Your brain's search engine and self-talk shape what you notice and how you respond to circumstances.
- When you feed your faith, your fears begin to starve.
- Believe systems are contagious. They spread throughout teams and organizations.

Reflection Questions

- How has your self-talk been shaping your daily actions? Are you reinforcing belief in yourself or feeding doubt?
- What are you currently training your brain to notice? Are you focusing more on obstacles or opportunities?
- If you were to describe your current mindset, would you call it fixed- or growth-oriented? What's one adjustment you could make to lean more into growth?
- When fear surfaces, what internal messages do you listen to? How might you intentionally shift toward reinforcing faith in your progress?

Practice Prompt

Before moving on, take one small step: Choose one belief about yourself or your team that you want to strengthen. Write it down, and for the next week, intentionally notice moments that reinforce this belief. As you do, pay attention to what changes in your focus, your energy, and your actions. Small shifts in attention can build stronger belief systems over time.

What's Next

In Chapter 3, we will review part of the materials list that is required to build a great team, which involves understanding the human drivers that either improve or diminish the engagement of others.

BLUEPRINT COMPONENT:
BUILDING MATERIALS

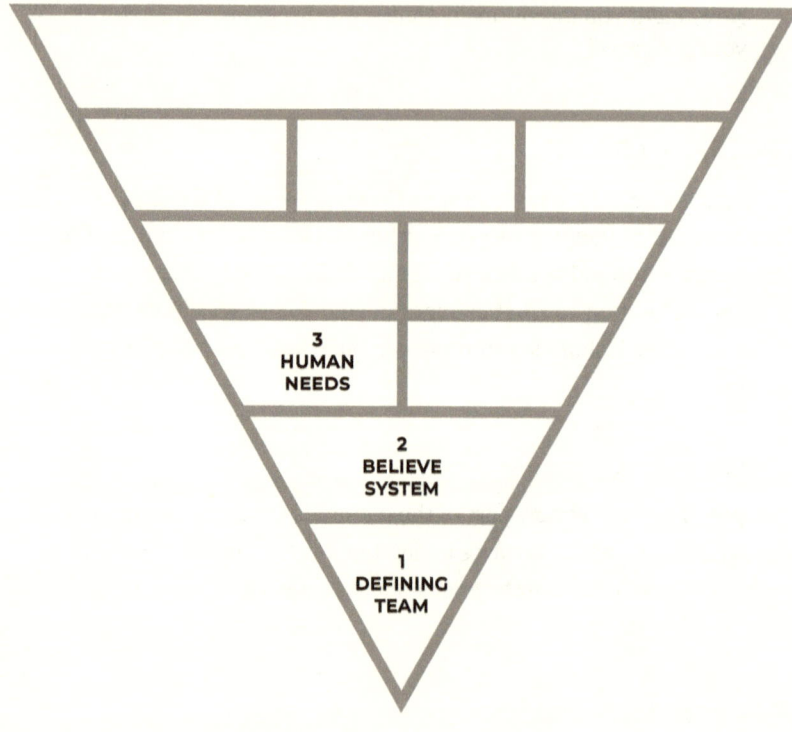

CHAPTER 3
THE NEEDS MODEL:
A FOUNDATION FOR STRONGER TEAMS, FAMILIES, AND RELATIONSHIPS

"He who knows others is wise;
he who knows himself is enlightened."

– LAO TZU

I once worked with an athletic team that had all the talent they needed to succeed. Individual players were skilled, physically prepared, and committed to winning. But something was systematically destroying their performance, and it wasn't their abilities.

The coach was creating an environment that violated every core human need. Players were pitted against teammates, moved to unfamiliar positions without explanation, publicly humiliated for mistakes, and never knew which version of their coach would show up each day. Despite their talent, they played cautiously, focused on self-preservation instead of team success.

That experience reminded me of something crucial: Teams don't fail because people lack ability; they fail because fundamental human needs aren't being met. When those needs are satisfied, people thrive. When they're neglected, even the most talented individuals withdraw.

The difference between teams that thrive under pressure and those that collapse is rarely about talent or resources. It comes down to whether core human needs are being met. Needs like belonging, respect, and fairness shape the way people show up, and when they are ignored, teams break down.

When these needs are satisfied, they promote commitment, engagement, and collaboration. When they're unmet, they create disengagement, or worse, active disengagement. People aren't just showing up for a paycheck, a win-loss record, or family obligations. What they're really showing up for is connection, equal treatment, respect, empowerment, and stability. When these needs are met, people don't just show up; they engage, they invest, and they thrive.

The NEEDS Framework Explained

Having observed teams across businesses, sports, and families, I've provided five researched core needs that help determine whether people engage fully or quietly withdraw. I call them NEEDS: Network, Empowerment, Equal treatment, Dignity, and Stability.

This isn't abstract theory. It's a real-world roadmap for creating environments where people want to succeed, not just environments where they're expected to succeed. These well-researched concepts—from Maslow's hierarchy to self-determination theory to psychological trust research and David Rock's SCARF model—consistently show that people thrive when they feel connected, empowered, fairly treated, valued, and secure. The NEEDS Model brings this understanding into daily practice.

For coaches, understanding these needs helps create engaged, high-performing teams that collaborate rather than compete. Managers who recognize these needs foster better workplace relationships and personal development. For parents, meeting these needs in their children builds confidence, resilience, and independence. For couples, satisfying these needs builds trust, engagement, and loyalty.

When you consistently meet people's core NEEDS, you compound toward connection, trust, and engagement. When you neglect these needs, even unintentionally, you drift toward disconnection and disengagement.

Network: The Power of Connection

When I talk about Network, I'm talking about the human need for connection. We are wired to belong. I often tell the teams and leaders I work with: No matter what the mission or culture looks like on the outside, people still crave the feeling of belonging on the inside. Connection is a universal human driver.

Connection often gets buried under urgency and deadlines, but it's the foundation that makes everything else possible. When people feel genuinely connected to their team, they contribute more freely, collaborate more effectively, and trust more deeply. Without connection, people work in isolation, hold back ideas, and focus on individual survival rather than collective success.

> Connection often gets buried under urgency and deadlines, but it's the foundation that makes everything else possible.

Teams with strong connection weather challenges better because members know they can rely on each other. They share information more openly, admit mistakes without fear, and step up when others need help. Connection transforms a group of individuals into a potentially great team. It is another element required to make the shift from accountability to ownership.

VIRTUAL CONNECTION CHALLENGES

In hybrid and remote environments, connection naturally requires more intentional effort because the casual interactions that build relationships don't happen accidentally. The hallway conversations, shared coffee breaks, and spontaneous check-ins that create bonds in traditional office settings must be deliberately re-created in digital spaces.

Virtual team leaders who excel at building connection understand they must design what used to happen organically. They create virtual coffee chats, use collaboration platforms for informal communication, begin meetings with personal check-ins, and establish online spaces where team members can share updates about their lives outside of work. The fundamental need for connection remains the same, but the delivery methods require more purposeful planning in distributed environments.

BUILDING CONNECTION IN LEADERSHIP

In the workplace, leaders who prioritize connection make it a point to see and acknowledge contributions. They schedule regular one-on-ones not just for status updates, but to understand what motivates each person. They create informal opportunities like team lunches, brief check-ins, or simply asking "How are you really doing?" that signal genuine care beyond productivity metrics.

Satya Nadella, the CEO of Microsoft, is a powerful example of this. He has reshaped the culture at Microsoft by leading with empathy and creating an environment where people feel heard, valued, and inspired to contribute fully. Nadella's leadership proves that when leaders focus on connection, they unlock not only engagement but also innovation and resilience.

CONNECTION IN COACHING AND PARENTING

Coaches build connection by fostering shared purpose, recognizing individual contributions, and building traditions that strengthen team identity. John Wooden, the legendary UCLA basketball coach, exemplified this approach. While he led his teams to ten NCAA championships, his focus was never solely on winning. Wooden prioritized character, personal growth, and building strong relationships with his players. He famously said, "I'm not coaching for championships; I'm coaching to help these young men become the best version of themselves." His players often reflected that it was Wooden's care for who they were off the court that inspired them to give everything they had on it.

PARENTING AND CONNECTION

Parents strengthen connection by being fully present in their children's lives, creating meaningful family moments, and showing consistent interest in what matters to their kids.

Dr. John Gottman calls these small moments "bids for connection." They occur when a child reaches out for attention, even in minor ways. How a parent responds in these moments builds emotional security and strengthens the family bond. A child might share an observation about a cloud, show excitement about a drawing, or simply want to sit nearby. Each response either reinforces or weakens the connection.

It's not the grand gestures that matter most; it's the daily, ordinary moments of attention and care that shape a child's sense of belonging and worth.

THE ONE PERCENT DRIFT IN CONNECTION

Connection follows the One Percent Rule perfectly. Small daily choices either build belonging or create distance. Choosing to really listen when someone shares an idea instead of half-listening while checking email. Taking thirty seconds to acknowledge someone's effort instead of rushing to the next task. Asking "How was your weekend?" and actually caring about the answer instead of treating it as small talk.

These micro-moments seem insignificant, but they compound. Teams that consistently choose connection over convenience develop unshakeable bonds. Teams that regularly prioritize task over relationship slowly drift into isolation, even when people sit side by side.

WHEN CONNECTION BREAKS DOWN

Just as certain behaviors build connection, there are subtle actions that quietly erode it. For leaders, it's focusing so heavily on results that people feel like cogs in a machine, cancelling one-on-ones, or recognizing only team achievements while individual contributions go unnoticed. For coaches, it's zeroing in on stats while overlooking effort, giving attention primarily to star athletes, or using sarcasm that chips away at trust. For parents and partners, it's being physically present but mentally checked out, missing small bids for connection, or letting conversations become transactional instead of relational.

What's consistent across these examples is that they're easy to miss. But over time, they send an unmistakable signal: You're not a priority. Awareness is our first defense. Small, consistent actions compound into deep, lasting trust.

Empowerment: The Control People Crave

Across every environment—the workplace, a sports team, within our families, or in our closest personal relationships—the need for empowerment is the same. We all want to feel trusted to make decisions and have ownership over our actions.

This is something I often bring up when I work with teams: Most of us don't like being told what to do, unless we truly don't know what we're doing or where we're going. And even then, once we have direction, we still want to feel like we have some control over how we get there. Empowerment is about balance.

Self-determination theory shows that autonomy is one of our core psychological needs. Without it, motivation fades. When people feel trusted and have meaningful choices, they become more engaged, more creative, and more committed. Whether you're at home, at work, on the field, or in your closest relationships, empowerment moves people from passive compliance to active ownership.

EMPOWERMENT IN REMOTE ENVIRONMENTS

Remote work naturally increases autonomy in some ways, but some team members may need more structure and check-ins to feel empowered rather than isolated. The key is understanding that empowerment in virtual environments looks different to different people. Some thrive with complete flexibility over their schedule and approach. Others need more frequent touchpoints and clearer guidelines to feel confident and supported rather than abandoned.

Effective virtual leaders ask questions like "What level of check-in feels supportive without feeling controlling?" and "What information do you need to feel confident making decisions independently?" They recognize that empowerment in remote settings requires finding the balance between giving people autonomy and providing the support structure they need to succeed.

EMPOWERMENT IN PRACTICE

In the workplace, empowerment shows up when a manager asks, "How would you approach this challenge?" instead of immediately providing the solution. Consider the difference between a leader who says, "Here's exactly how to handle this client situation," versus one who says, "You know this client well. What approach do you think would work best? I'm here if you need to brainstorm." The second approach empowers the employee to think critically, take ownership, and grow their problem-solving skills, while still providing support.

This same principle applies in coaching and parenting. Coaches who ask players "What did you see on that play?" before giving feedback help athletes develop game awareness and decision-making skills. Parents who involve children in age-appropriate decisions, from choosing weekend activities to planning family meals, build confidence and responsibility.

THE ONE PERCENT DRIFT IN EMPOWERMENT

Empowerment erodes or grows through daily choices about control and trust. Asking for someone's input instead of dictating the approach. Letting people figure out solutions instead of jumping in with answers.

Trusting people to handle responsibilities instead of checking in every hour.

Each choice to trust instead of control builds empowerment by one percent. Each choice to micromanage instead of guide erodes it by one percent. Over time, these small decisions create either an environment where people take ownership and initiative, or one where people wait to be told what to do.

THE HIDDEN COST OF MICROMANAGEMENT

Unfortunately, many well-intentioned leaders, coaches, and parents unintentionally limit empowerment. For leaders, it's micromanaging tasks, always supplying solutions instead of inviting ideas, or overriding decisions. For coaches, it's dictating every move, focusing only on execution instead of encouraging players to read and adapt, or correcting immediately rather than letting players self-assess. For parents and partners, it's making decisions for the other in areas where they could choose, stepping in too quickly to "fix" problems, or offering constant direction that feels like control rather than care.

These actions send the wrong message: *I don't fully trust you to handle this.* Empowerment isn't about stepping back completely; it's about stepping alongside others and giving them space to step forward with ownership and confidence.

Equal Treatment: The Fairness Factor

Equal treatment matters everywhere. People pay close attention to it. They might not always speak up about it, but they notice when recognition, opportunity, or responsibilities don't seem to match the effort being put in.

This attention to equal treatment is hardwired in us. Researchers Blake and McAuliffe found that even young children, before they can fully explain their feelings, show strong emotional responses to unfair situations. Our sense of fairness shows up early and never really leaves us. It's like a built-in alert system that tells us when trust is at risk.

Organizational justice theory highlights that equal treatment is about more than just outcomes; it's about how decisions are made and how people are treated along the way. People don't just want a fair result;

they want to know the process is fair and that they've been treated with respect.

The thing about equal treatment is that it isn't about treating everyone exactly the same. It's about making sure people feel that what they bring to the table is genuinely considered. People don't expect perfection, but they do expect fairness.

In hybrid environments, equal treatment requires extra attention, because proximity bias can unintentionally favor office workers over remote team members. Leaders may unconsciously give more attention, opportunities, or recognition to people they see in person regularly, while remote workers feel less visible and less included in important decisions or casual conversations that shape team dynamics.

Effective hybrid leaders actively counteract this by ensuring virtual team members get equal speaking time in meetings, equal access to growth opportunities, equal recognition for their contributions, and equal inclusion in both formal and informal team communications. They develop systems to track and ensure fairness across both in-person and remote team members.

A REAL ORGANIZATION'S WAKE-UP CALL

One organization I worked with discovered that their "open door" policy wasn't as equal as they thought. While leadership genuinely welcomed input from anyone, more assertive personalities were comfortable walking into offices and sharing ideas, while quieter team members felt hesitant to interrupt busy executives. The result was unintentional favoritism toward those who spoke up, while valuable perspectives from thoughtful, reserved employees went unheard.

Once leadership recognized this pattern, they implemented structured feedback sessions and anonymous suggestion systems to ensure everyone's voice had equal access to decision makers. This simple change transformed how decisions were made and how people felt about their ability to contribute.

THE ONE PERCENT DRIFT IN EQUAL TREATMENT

Equal treatment builds or erodes through seemingly small choices about attention and opportunity. Asking for input from the quiet person in the meeting instead of only hearing from the vocal ones. Giving recognition to the person who does steady work instead of only celebrating the dramatic wins. Explaining decisions instead of assuming people understand the reasoning.

These micro-choices about inclusion and fairness compound over time. Teams that consistently choose inclusive practices develop cultures where everyone feels valued. Teams that regularly default to convenient patterns slowly create inner circles and outer circles, even when it's unintentional.

WHEN FAIRNESS GETS COMPROMISED

What's tricky about equal treatment is that it's often undermined by accident. At work, it's continuously giving high-profile tasks to the same people because they're reliable, overlooking quiet contributors in discussions, or failing to explain decisions about promotions. On teams, it's focusing coaching attention mostly on star players, not giving effort the same weight as talent, or missing opportunities to involve every player meaningfully. In families, it's holding different standards for siblings without realizing it or assuming one partner will naturally carry more emotional load.

What these have in common is that they often start with good intentions: efficiency, ease, or habit. But they can quietly erode trust if we're not mindful. Equal treatment is about making sure people feel seen, considered, and valued based on their effort, contribution, and situation.

Dignity: Making People Matter

We all want to feel like we matter. Whether we're at work, on a team, in our family, or in our closest relationships, feeling seen and respected is essential to staying engaged and motivated. Dignity isn't about flattery or empty praise; it's about genuine acknowledgment of people's value, effort, and presence.

When people feel respected, they show up more fully. When they don't, they quietly withdraw. Dignity is built, or eroded, in the small, everyday moments that tell people, "You matter here."

Considerable research on psychological trust reveals that people perform at their best when they feel safe and respected.

> When people feel respected, they show up more fully. When they don't, they quietly withdraw.

When dignity is present, people are more likely to contribute, share ideas, and stay engaged.

In remote and hybrid environments, demonstrating respect and appreciation requires more intentional effort, because casual recognition opportunities that are available when working in the same location are not available. The quick "thank you" in the hallway, the nod of appreciation during a meeting, or the informal acknowledgment of someone's contribution becomes less visible in virtual settings.

DIGNITY IN DAILY LEADERSHIP

In the workplace, dignity shows up when leaders acknowledge the behind-the-scenes work that keeps teams running smoothly: the administrative assistant who anticipates needs, the engineer who stays late to prevent a problem, or the customer-service representative who de-escalates a difficult situation. When leaders consistently express gratitude for these everyday efforts, they signal that all work has value and that every person's presence matters.

At work, it's about recognizing effort, not just outcomes. On a team, it's about showing respect for every role, not just the ones in the spotlight. In families, it's about listening with attention, even when the topic seems small. In personal relationships, small acts of appreciation and respect are key ingredients in long-term connection and trust.

Dignity accumulates through small daily acknowledgments or erodes through small daily oversights. Saying thank you for the routine work instead of only celebrating the exceptional. Acknowledging someone's presence when they join a conversation instead of continuing without pause. Noticing effort, even when the results aren't perfect, instead of only recognizing success.

These tiny moments of recognition seem insignificant, but they signal to people whether they matter. Teams that consistently choose to see and acknowledge contributions develop cultures where people feel valued. Teams that regularly overlook everyday efforts slowly create environments where people feel invisible.

HOW A PERSON'S DIGNITY GETS UNDERMINED

Dignity can be undermined unintentionally. At work, it's focusing recognition only on visible wins while overlooking steady contributions, interrupting people's ideas in meetings, or assigning tasks without explaining their importance. On teams, it's overcelebrating star performers while ignoring supporting roles, not giving credit for effort and preparation, or missing opportunities to recognize contributions that aren't in the spotlight. In families and relationships, it's half-listening to daily stories, dismissing small successes, or taking for granted the consistent efforts that keep relationships strong.

These moments are usually not intended to harm; they're often the byproduct of distraction or routine. But over time, they send a message that a person's presence and effort are not fully valued. The good news is, restoring dignity is simple. It starts with noticing effort, presence, and contribution, then taking a moment to acknowledge it.

Stability: Predictability Under Pressure

Uncertainty creates stress. When people don't know what to expect, it eats away at focus and confidence. Neuroscientific research shows that uncertainty activates the brain's threat response system, making people more anxious and distracted. Predictability calms this system, helping people focus and engage fully. Stability doesn't mean avoiding change; it means providing predictability in the things that matter most: communication, expectations, and leadership.

Stability builds through consistent small actions or erodes through inconsistent patterns. Following through on commitments instead of letting things slide. Communicating changes ahead of time instead of springing surprises. Maintaining predictable behavior, even when you're stressed, instead of letting emotions dictate your responses. This becomes especially critical in virtual environments where teams lack the natural stability of shared physical presence. Without face-to-face interaction, remote teams rely heavily on predictable check-ins, reliable response patterns, and steady feedback loops to feel connected and secure.

Consider a sales team leader who holds a standing Monday morning call at 9 a.m. Every week, the team knows they'll get updates on priorities, hear about wins from the previous week, and align on the week ahead. The leader responds to questions within twenty-four hours and sends a brief Friday summary email highlighting progress and upcoming challenges. When unexpected changes happen, she communicates them immediately with context about why and what it means for the team. This predictability allows team members to plan their weeks, feel informed, and focus their energy on selling rather than wondering what's happening or feeling anxious about being left out of the loop. Over time, this consistency builds trust and psychological trust that translates directly into performance.

Instability often creeps in unintentionally. At work, it shows up as constantly shifting priorities without explanation, inconsistent communication, or leaders whose tone changes day to day. On teams, it's unclear roles, practices that start and stop unpredictably, or sporadic feedback. In families, it's rules that change without warning, broken promises, or emotional unpredictability. In relationships, it's inconsistent attention, mixed signals, or being emotionally available one moment and distant the next.

These patterns send a powerful message: You can't count on this. Over time, people respond by pulling back or disengaging entirely. The good news is that stability can be restored through small, deliberate actions like consistent communication, follow-through on commitments, and clear expectations.

To understand the full power of the NEEDS Model, consider what happens when every essential need goes unmet. The athletic team I mentioned earlier provides a stark example of systematic failure across all five areas. Rather than fostering unity, the coach pitted players against each other, encouraging unhealthy competition within the team. Players focused on self-preservation instead of team success, eroding trust and connection. They were moved into unfamiliar positions without explanation or preparation, then yelled at to "control their behavior" when they struggled. Favoritism was rampant. Certain players received preferential treatment while others, despite equal or greater effort, were overlooked or unfairly criticized. Players were regularly berated in front of teammates, publicly called out in ways that left them feeling humiliated and small. Perhaps worst of all, the coach's behavior was completely unpredictable. Some days calm and supportive, other days volatile and explosive. Players never knew which version would show up, creating constant anxiety and uncertainty.

This environment left every need unmet. Without Connection, Empowerment, Equal treatment, Dignity, and Stability, the players' motivation and commitment unraveled. They showed up physically but not mentally or emotionally. Despite having all the talent necessary to succeed, they underperformed because their fundamental human NEEDS were being systematically violated. This is the One Percent Rule in reverse: daily choices that undermined every core need compounded into complete team dysfunction. What started as individual coaching decisions accumulated into a culture where talented players couldn't perform to their potential.

THE PERFORMANCE-REVIEW EXAMPLE

The same dynamics play out in offices every day. I once worked with an employee who walked into what they assumed would be a routine performance review, only to be blindsided by unexpectedly negative feedback. There had been no prior conversations, no indicators of concern, and no opportunity to course-correct. Nearly every essential need was left unmet.

The employee already felt a weak sense of connection with their manager. Without regular check-ins, the relationship lacked depth and trust, so the performance review felt cold and transactional rather than part of an ongoing, supportive relationship. They felt powerless because there had been no earlier discussions or feedback, no opportunity to adjust their performance or influence the outcome. Decisions about their future felt entirely out of their hands. What stung most was learning they were being evaluated on criteria they hadn't even known were part of their performance expectations. It felt unfair and arbitrary, as though the rules had changed without notice. Hearing their performance described as poor, without prior warning or recognition of their efforts, left them feeling devalued and underappreciated. Their hard work had gone unnoticed, and their dignity took a direct hit. The conversation left them deeply unsettled about their future. Without clarity or confidence in their standing, they began to worry about job security. This uncertainty created lingering anxiety that followed them well beyond the meeting.

What happened in that single conversation is a powerful reminder: When people's core NEEDS are neglected, the damage extends beyond that moment. It impacts motivation, trust, and future engagement.

Whether in an office, on a team, or at home, unmet NEEDS widen the gap between what people are capable of and what they're willing to give. This demonstrates the One Percent Rule's destructive power: months of small oversights, missed connections, and unclear communication accumulated into one conversation that damaged the relationship and the employee's engagement permanently.

Key Takeaways

- The NEEDS Model applies universally across leadership, coaching, parenting, and relationships. The five core needs (Network, Empowerment, Equal treatment, Dignity, and Stability) are always at play. When met, people engage fully. When neglected, motivation erodes.

- The One Percent Rule applies powerfully to human needs. Small daily choices to meet or neglect these needs compound over time into either thriving relationships or dysfunctional ones.

- Virtual and hybrid environments amplify the importance of meeting needs intentionally, as casual opportunities for connection, fairness, and stability require deliberate design.

- Neglect is often unintentional but equally damaging. Awareness is your first defense. You don't have to be perfect; you have to be intentional. Small actions compound over time.

- Teams don't fail because of lack of talent; they fail when fundamental human needs aren't met. The most skilled individuals will withdraw when their needs for connection, fairness, respect, autonomy, and predictability are violated.

Reflection Questions

- **Network:** Who might be feeling disconnected? What can I do today to strengthen their belonging?
- **Empowerment:** Am I giving people space to make decisions, or controlling outcomes?
- **Equal treatment:** Am I unintentionally favoring some people over others?
- **Dignity:** Do I consistently acknowledge effort and contributions from everyone?
- **Stability:** Am I providing predictable communication and clear expectations?

In hybrid or remote settings, how am I ensuring all five NEEDS are met across both in-person and virtual team members?

What one percent choices am I making daily that either meet or neglect people's core NEEDS?

Practice Prompt

Choose one of the five NEEDS and identify someone whose need in that area might not be fully met. This week, intentionally practice the CABLES Behaviors (Chapter 4) that support that need. Notice how small, consistent actions begin to address fundamental human needs and strengthen your relationships. Pay attention to the one percent compound effect: how small daily choices to meet people's needs build stronger connections over time.

The Foundation for Everything That Follows

Understanding the NEEDS Model and practicing CABLES Behaviors creates the foundation for building great teams. But before we explore how teams support, celebrate, and challenge each other, we need to address a fundamental truth: you cannot consistently give if you haven't developed yourself personally.

In the next chapter, we will discuss the specific CABLES Behaviors that satisfy the NEEDS that were outline in this chapter. These behaviors are part of the essential building materials required to build the missing piece great teams share: ownership.

BLUEPRINT COMPONENT:
BUILDING MATERIALS

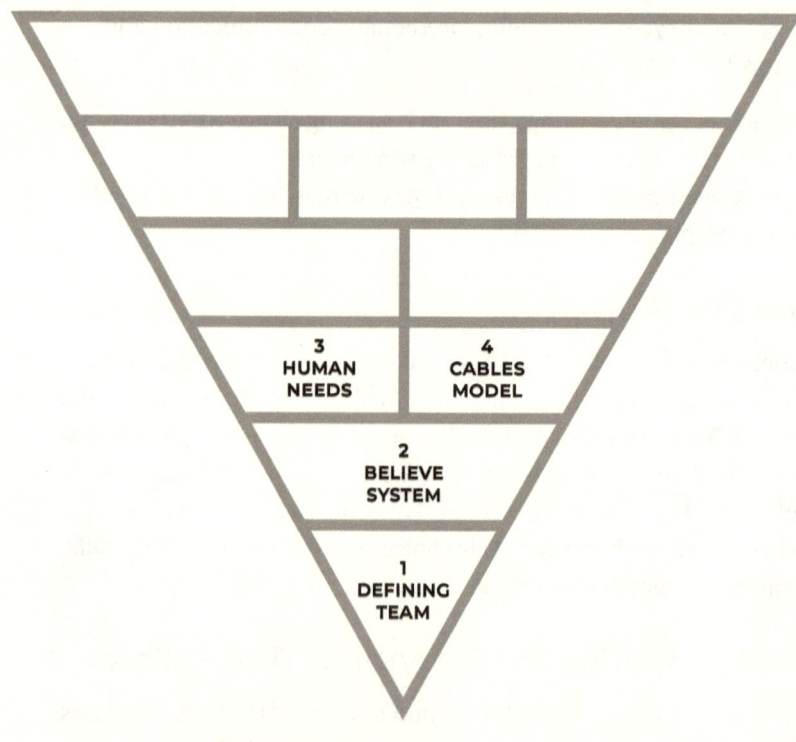

CHAPTER 4
BUILDING THE BRIDGES
THAT CARRY TEAMS TO SUCCESS

*"Our behaviors will either build bridges or barriers
with those around us."*

–ANON

"I simply don't have the time to connect regularly with my employees or players."

I hear this from managers and coaches constantly. My answer is always the same: You don't have time not to.

No team rises above the strength of its relationships. While belief in ourselves shapes how we show up, it's the bonds between team members that determine how far we go together. Great teams aren't accidents. They're built intentionally, one strong connection at a time. And if your goal is to build a great team, whether in the workplace, on the field, or at home, connection isn't optional. It's the foundation, and it can't occur without commitment.

I saw this play out recently with a large organization where projects stretched over years. People were frustrated, constantly reminded of how much work remained instead of recognizing progress already made. Then something shifted. Leaders in our workshops decided to pay more attention to celebrating milestones and acknowledging what had been accomplished along the way. Their team's energy changed almost immediately. People seemed more motivated to complete their assignments and more willing to speak up about how work processes could be improved. A small change in behavior created a measurable difference in engagement.

How CABLES Build the Strongest Relationship Bridges

Every relationship within a team functions like a bridge. Some are sturdy and resilient, built to handle pressure and navigate conflict. Others, left weak or neglected, collapse under the weight of miscommunication and mistrust. When bridges are fragile, even small challenges feel overwhelming. But when bridges are strong, teams face adversity head-on, hold each other to high standards, and support one another without fear of collapse.

Just like physical bridges, not all relationship bridges are built the same way. Some are hastily constructed with minimum effort and crumble under strain. Others are engineered to bear heavy weight, reinforced over time, and maintained with care. The encouraging truth? Regardless of where you start, any bridge can be strengthened.

After studying hundreds of high-performing relationships across businesses, sports, and families, I've identified six specific behaviors that consistently strengthen connections. They don't happen by accident, and they don't require special talent. They require intention and consistency. Think of them as the cables that give bridges their strength. Remove any one, and the whole structure weakens. Practice all six consistently, and you build relationships that can withstand any pressure.

These six behaviors are another essential set of building materials for your master blueprint. In the previous chapters, we explored the foundation of a believe system and the framework of NEEDS. Now we add the connecting elements that bring everything together.

I call them CABLES: Consistency, Appreciation, Belongingness, Listening, Empathy, and Specificity.

Think of your team's relationships like a suspension bridge built from CABLES Behaviors. Every time you demonstrate Consistency, Appreciation, Belongingness, Listening, Empathy, and Specificity, you add another wire to the structure. Over time, these behaviors don't just hold the bridge together; they increase its capacity to carry greater weight.

In my first book, *The Leadership Bridge*, I used the Golden Gate Bridge as a metaphor for how relationships are built one meaningful behavior at a time. That bridge's two massive cables, each made of over 27,000 individual wires, illustrate a powerful truth: On their own, each wire is weak, but bound together, they create extraordinary strength.

The same is true for the behaviors that form high-trust relationships. Each time we show consistency, offer appreciation, or genuinely listen, we add another wire to the bridge, increasing its capacity to carry the weight of real-life challenges.

> Strong bridges and strong teams aren't built in a day. They're built one cable at a time.

Strong bridges and strong teams aren't built in a day. They're built one cable at a time.

Here's how.

Consistency: The Foundation of Trust

Consistency is the foundation of any great team. Without it, trust erodes, expectations become unclear, and relationships weaken under pressure. Teams thrive when members can rely on one another, when actions align with words, and when commitments are met with follow-through. In its simplest terms, consistency is nothing more than "walking the talk." It's a constant opportunity to look in the mirror and ask, "Am I holding myself to the same standards and expectations I have for those around me?"

In hybrid and remote environments, consistency becomes even more critical because teammates can't observe your daily behavior patterns. Your punctuality to virtual meetings, response time to messages, and follow-through on digital commitments become the primary consistency signals people use to evaluate your reliability. When someone consistently joins video calls a few minutes late or regularly responds to emails days after receiving them, these small inconsistencies compound faster in virtual settings because there aren't casual hallway interactions to offset the negative impressions.

WALKING THE TALK: A PERSONAL EXAMPLE

Consistency means showing up physically, emotionally, and intellectually the same way every time. It's about holding the same expectations for everyone, including ourselves. But it's harder than it sounds, and I learned this lesson the hard way through my own parenting.

I can't lecture my children about safe driving if, when they're in the car with me, I'm flying down the highway at 80 miles an hour flipping through emails. They won't hear my words; they'll see my actions. My inconsistency teaches them more loudly than any speech I could give.

The same principle applies everywhere. I can't tell my team that work-life balance matters while sending emails at 11 p.m. and expecting immediate responses. I can't emphasize the importance of preparation while showing up to meetings unprepared myself. I can't preach open communication while shutting down ideas I disagree with or checking my phone when someone's talking to me.

This gap between what we say and what we do is where trust begins to erode in every relationship. People don't just listen to our words; they watch our patterns. They notice when we hold them to standards we don't follow ourselves. If I expect high levels of follow-through from my team, I must hold myself to the same standard. When I fall short and expect understanding for my inconsistencies but don't offer it to others, I quietly dismantle the trust that holds my relationships together. Every time we ask others to do what we won't do ourselves, we add another crack to the bridge we're trying to build.

CONSISTENCY IN LEADERSHIP

Research supports this principle. Studies show that when individuals perceive their leaders as consistent, they are more likely to be motivated and committed to their work. Without consistency, doubt and uncertainty creep in, leading to disengagement and decreased performance.

Consider a manager who holds regular one-on-one check-ins, provides clear feedback, and reliably follows up on team goals. This creates psychological trust, where team members feel secure and engaged. They can plan their work around predictable touchpoints and trust that their manager will be there when needed. In contrast, when leadership changes targets and expectations week to week without explanation, employees feel like they're aiming at a moving target, resulting in frustration and poor performance. They become hesitant to commit fully because they've learned that priorities might shift before they finish their current work.

In virtual team settings, this becomes even more critical. Without the natural consistency that comes from sharing physical space, distributed teams rely almost entirely on predictable patterns to feel connected. The manager who maintains consistent virtual office hours, responds to messages within agreed-upon time frames, and holds regular team meetings creates stability that helps remote workers feel less isolated and more aligned. What might seem like minor schedule shifts in a traditional office can feel destabilizing when your only connection to the team is through a screen.

In sports, consistency shows up in the athlete who is always first to practice, hustles on every play, and maintains a positive attitude regardless of the scoreboard. This reliability becomes a standard others measure themselves against. But when coaches or players are inconsistent, the consequences are immediate and visible. A coach who preaches mental discipline and then loses control when things go wrong sees their message collapse under hypocrisy. Players learn to discount what the coach says because actions have proven words meaningless. The trust cable starts to fray, and once players stop believing in their coach's consistency, performance suffers.

BUILDING CONSISTENT HABITS

Within families, consistency creates the stable environment children need to thrive. Parents who maintain clear boundaries, such as regular bedtimes or screen-time limits, foster security, even when those rules aren't popular. Children know what to expect, which paradoxically gives them the freedom to explore and take risks elsewhere, because they trust the foundation won't shift beneath them.

The same dynamic plays out in personal relationships. A friend who consistently checks in, keeps promises, and is emotionally available becomes a source of deep trust. You know you can count on them in a crisis because they've proven reliable in ordinary moments. Contrast that with a romantic partner whose attention and care swing unpredictably between intense engagement and distant withdrawal. This unpredictability creates constant anxiety, leaving you unsure where you stand and whether the relationship can be trusted.

Consider a team where deadlines are treated as suggestions, expectations shift without warning, and commitments aren't honored. The result is frustration, inefficiency, and broken trust. People stop relying on one another, because experience has taught them that follow-through is optional. Collaboration becomes transactional rather than collaborative, with everyone protecting themselves first. Now picture a team where consistency is a shared value. Everyone knows what's expected, communication is steady, and follow-through is reliable. Trust deepens because people can plan around each other's commitments. Collaboration thrives because the foundation is solid enough to support risk taking and innovation.

Just like a well-built bridge, a strong team depends on consistency in every supporting cable to carry the weight of responsibility, communication, and trust. When consistency is practiced across all interactions, it creates an environment where people can do their best work, knowing they are supported by a reliable foundation that won't suddenly shift beneath them.

Appreciation: The Fuel for Motivation

Appreciation is more than recognizing effort. It's about valuing people for both who they are and what they do. Teams are made up of individuals with different backgrounds, perspectives, and strengths. Great teams don't just tolerate these differences, they appreciate and embrace them. When people feel seen and valued, not only for their performance but for their presence, they are more engaged, motivated, and committed to the team's success.

THE THREE-PART RECOGNITION FORMULA

There are two essential ways to strengthen this cable in your relationship bridge. The first is recognizing people for who they are: their character, their quiet strengths, their loyalty, their humor, their reliability. This kind of recognition reaches deeper than performance alone. It tells the person: You matter, not just what you produce.

The second is recognizing people for what they do: their efforts, their persistence, and their accomplishments. But this is where many leaders miss the mark. Too often, recognition is vague and generic. Telling someone "great job" or "you're a rockstar" is a nice start, but it lacks impact if you don't tell them what, specifically, they did well.

To make recognition most effective, I use a simple, three-part approach. First, make it meaningful. Tailor appreciation to what matters to the individual. One great way to do this is to simply ask: "Can you tell me about a time you were recognized in a way that stuck with you?" Their answer will give you valuable insight into how they like to be appreciated.

Second, make it specific. Describe exactly what they did that deserves recognition. Specific feedback is remembered because it reinforces the behavior clearly.

Last, make it unexpected. Neuroscience shows that when appreciation is unexpected, it creates a stronger dopamine response in the brain. Dopamine, the brain's reward chemical, spikes when positive reinforcement is a surprise. In contrast, when recognition is expected but doesn't arrive, dopamine levels actually drop, leading to feelings of frustration and discouragement.

In hybrid and remote environments, creating meaningful appreciation requires additional intentionality because positive moments become less visible. The team member who stays late to help a colleague might go unnoticed when everyone works from different locations. The problem solved between virtual meetings doesn't get seen by others. Digital appreciation systems, video recognition messages, and virtual celebration rituals become essential tools for maintaining the recognition that keeps teams engaged.

Remote leaders who excel at appreciation are more systematic about it. They schedule regular recognition in team meetings, use collaboration platforms to highlight contributions publicly, and find creative ways to make appreciation feel personal, even through digital channels. They understand that in virtual environments, if recognition isn't intentionally planned, it often doesn't happen at all.

WHY RECOGNITION TRANSFORMS TEAMS

In one large organization I worked with, projects had long timelines, sometimes stretching over years. People were getting frustrated. They were constantly reminded of how much was left to do, which kept their focus locked on the gap between where they were and where they needed to be. Progress felt invisible.

I suggested they find ways to recognize what had already been accomplished along the way. Celebrate milestones. Acknowledge the progress, even if it wasn't the final destination. This small shift changed the energy of the team. People started to see their progress, not just the gap, and motivation increased.

THE HIDDEN COST OF MISSING RECOGNITION

I often reference the concept of gap versus gain when working with leaders. This ties directly into powerful insights from *The Gap and The Gain* by Dan Sullivan and Dr. Benjamin Hardy. People are naturally wired to notice what's missing, the gap between where they are and where they want to be. But when we train ourselves and our teams to recognize the gain, to celebrate effort and progress rather than focusing only on outcomes, we build momentum.

The neuroscience behind this is compelling. When we focus only on the gap, we're likely reducing dopamine levels in the brain, which directly impacts engagement and motivation. People feel like they're constantly falling short, never quite measuring up. Over time, this creates a spiral of disengagement. But when we find ways to recognize the gain, we improve engagement by triggering dopamine increases. Recognition literally changes brain chemistry in ways that fuel continued effort and connection.

In my experience across organizations, the absence of appreciation is more common than most leaders realize. There are people in almost every workplace who are quietly putting in enormous effort, yet they don't even hear a simple "thank you." They feel invisible. When appreciation is absent or when people feel their efforts go unnoticed, dopamine levels don't just stay neutral; they decline. The person who consistently delivers quality work but never receives acknowledgment eventually stops going the extra mile. Why would they? Their brain has learned that effort doesn't register, doesn't matter.

Recognition, in these cases, is the lowest-hanging fruit for improving engagement and motivation. It costs nothing, yet delivers enormous returns. But it requires shifting from gap-focused thinking to gain-focused awareness. Instead of only noticing what didn't get done or what could have been better, we train ourselves to see what did get accomplished, what effort was invested, what progress was made.

Modeling appreciation means going beyond surface-level gestures. It's the leader who doesn't wait for the formal performance review but catches effort in the moment and names it specifically. It's the coworker who notices the small, meaningful contributions that keep the team moving forward; the person who stayed late to help a colleague or caught an error before it became a problem. It's the parent or friend who expresses gratitude not just for tasks completed but for the qualities of character that enrich the relationship, acknowledging patience, kindness, persistence, or courage when they see it.

Just like a suspension bridge needs strong cables to bear weight, a great team or relationship relies on appreciation to maintain connection and resilience. When appreciation becomes part of the culture, when people are recognized for their gains rather than only measured against the gap, relationships strengthen, morale rises, and teams achieve greater success together.

Belongingness: Creating Connection That Matters

When people feel they are part of something larger than themselves, they contribute more freely, collaborate more effectively, and trust more deeply. A strong sense of belonging fosters an environment where individuals are willing to take risks, share ideas, and support one another through challenges. Without it, teams struggle with disengagement, exclusion, and declining morale.

In my conversations with managers and coaches over the years, this comes up again and again. They often tell me they simply don't have the time to connect regularly with their employees or players. My answer is always the same: You don't have time not to. If your goal is to build a great team—whether in the workplace, on the field, or at home—connection is not optional. It is the foundation.

Without frequent, meaningful, and positive interactions, relationships weaken. This applies just as much in families and personal relationships as it does in professional ones. If we aren't making time for proximity and positive intensity, we are unintentionally allowing distance and disengagement to grow. The problem isn't usually that leaders don't value connection; it's that they underestimate how quickly its absence erodes the team they're trying to build.

Virtual environments make this even more challenging, requiring leaders to be more intentional about creating belonging. The casual conversations that naturally build relationships in traditional office settings simply don't happen when everyone works from separate spaces.

There's no hallway chat, no impromptu lunch conversation, no moment after a meeting where someone shares what's really going on. Digital team leaders who successfully create belonging understand they must deliberately design what used to happen by accident.

This might mean starting meetings with personal check-ins, creating virtual coffee-chat opportunities, scheduling online team-building activities, or establishing digital spaces where team members can share personal updates and celebrate each other's lives outside of work. The principle remains the same: proximity, frequency, duration, and positive intensity of interaction. But in hybrid environments, each element requires more purposeful planning. What once emerged naturally now demands intention, but the investment pays the same dividends in trust, engagement, and performance.

THE SCIENCE OF BELONGING

This isn't just intuition; it's deeply rooted in human biology. Neuroscientific research has shown that the brain experiences social exclusion and isolation as physical pain. The same neural pathways that process physical injury are activated when we feel left out. The cost of disconnection is real: It impacts morale and diminishes performance, creativity, and health.

I once worked with a manager who shared a story from a previous company. The majority of his team spoke both French and English, but he only spoke English. When the group went to lunch together, they naturally fell into speaking French. He understood they weren't intentionally excluding him, but he always felt alienated sitting there unable to participate in the conversation. Despite enjoying the work itself, he eventually decided to leave the company. The pain of daily exclusion outweighed his satisfaction with the job. His team likely never knew why he left, but the lack of belonging had made his position unsustainable.

Research published in *Harvard Business Review* found that individuals who feel a strong sense of belonging at work are significantly more likely to perform at a high level, experience lower stress, and demonstrate greater commitment to team goals. But when people don't feel included, they naturally withdraw. Collaboration fades, contributions decrease, and people emotionally check out long before they physically leave, just like that manager who spent months feeling disconnected before finally walking away.

Understanding how belonging is built helps us avoid this erosion. In the book *The Like Switch*, written by former FBI agent Dr. Jack Schafer and Dr. Marvin Karlins, they presented research that outlined four key factors that drive connection: proximity, frequency, duration, and intensity of interaction. Simply put, the more we are around people, the more frequently we interact; and the longer and more positively intense those interactions are, the stronger the relationship becomes.

But proximity alone isn't enough. If the intensity of those interactions is negative, filled with criticism, avoidance, or indifference, the closeness becomes corrosive rather than constructive. That manager sat in physical proximity to his team every day at lunch, with high frequency and duration, but the intensity was negative because he felt invisible and excluded. To build strong bridges of belonging, proximity and frequency must be paired with positive intensity: genuine engagement, warmth, curiosity, and respect.

BUILDING ACTIVE BELONGING

Modeling belongingness means being intentional about creating positive moments of connection. It's the leader who actively invites every voice to the conversation, not just the loudest ones. It's the teammate who notices when someone is on the fringe and draws them into the group. It's the organization that celebrates diverse backgrounds and experiences, seeing them not as barriers but as bridges to better solutions.

I've seen teams transform when they shift from passive inclusion to active belonging. Teams that once worked in silos began holding short, regular huddles, increasing proximity, frequency, and duration of their interactions in meaningful ways. They focused on the intensity of those moments, making space for recognition, sharing challenges openly, and expressing genuine curiosity about each other's experiences. The result was a noticeable rise in trust and collaboration.

Teams that ignore belongingness often slip into quiet disengagement. People attend meetings but remain silent. Ideas go unspoken because people fear judgment or indifference. Slowly, relationships weaken and trust erodes.

Belongingness is a structural cable in the bridge of human connection. When people feel like they belong, they engage more deeply, support one another more willingly, and contribute with greater energy and creativity. Just like the other cables in our relationship bridge, belonging requires consistent maintenance. It's not enough to assume people feel included; we have to build it intentionally, day after day.

Listening: Your Leadership Superpower

Authentic listening is one of the most powerful tools we have to strengthen relationships and build trust. I often describe it as a superpower because it has the ability to transform not just conversations, but entire teams and organizations. It is the foundation of meaningful communication and collaboration.

A SALES LESSON THAT CHANGED EVERYTHING

When I first started in sales, I learned a piece of advice that stuck with me: "You have one mouth and two ears, use them in that ratio." At the time, it seemed clever, but over the years, I've realized how profound it is for leadership, coaching, family, and friendships.

When we talk, we're just repeating what we already know. But when we listen, authentically listen, we give ourselves the opportunity to learn something new. In fact, it's only when we listen that we ever have the opportunity to learn something new. The longer we let someone speak, the more they may reveal, often telling us exactly what we need to know to understand their needs, their concerns, or how to solve a challenge together.

Authentic listening in virtual environments requires additional focus and intentionality. When communicating through screens, we must work harder to observe nonverbal cues, watch for signs of disengagement, and create space for voices that might get lost in virtual group dynamics. The leader who masters virtual listening learns to read energy levels through a camera, notices when someone wants to contribute but isn't speaking up, and adapts their listening approach to account for the unique dynamics of digital communication.

Technical elements also matter: ensuring good audio quality, minimizing distractions, using features like breakout rooms to create more intimate listening opportunities, and being especially attentive to tone and verbal cues when visual information is limited or unclear.

WHAT MAKES LISTENING AUTHENTIC

I believe authentic listening is a step above effective styles like active or reflective listening. While those methods have value, they can become mechanical tools for manipulation when used without genuine care. Someone might master the technical aspects like paraphrasing and maintaining eye contact while having entirely self-serving motives, appearing engaged while actually exploiting the interaction.

Authentic listening is different because it comes from genuine curiosity and respect, not just technique. It's about truly caring to understand the other person. When we listen authentically, we aren't performing behaviors; we are genuinely invested in what the other person has to say. This fundamental difference in intent creates a natural barrier against deceptive use, since you cannot simultaneously hold deep respect for someone and seek to deceive them.

THE FOUR COMPONENTS OF AUTHENTIC LISTENING

Authentic listening is composed of four essential components: listening with the eyes, the ears, the mind, and respect.

Listening with the eyes means being fully present in the conversation. It involves observing body language, facial expressions, and nonverbal cues that provide context beyond spoken words. A person who avoids eye contact or appears distracted sends the message that they might not be fully engaged, weakening trust and connection.

Listening with the ears is about more than just processing words. Tone, inflection, and emphasis provide critical insights into what someone is truly communicating. Paying attention to these subtleties allows a listener to pick up on underlying emotions, concerns, or excitement that might not be explicitly stated.

Listening with the mind requires curiosity and reflection. Instead of formulating a response while the other person is speaking, authentic listeners focus on understanding before reacting. They ask thoughtful questions, paraphrase key points to confirm understanding, and remain open to perspectives that challenge their assumptions. This mental discipline elevates listening from passive hearing to active discovery.

Listening with respect means treating the speaker with the same level of attentiveness one would want in return. This includes avoiding interruptions, resisting the urge to dismiss concerns, and creating space for honest dialogue. Respectful listening builds psychological trust, which is essential for collaboration and trust.

THE TRANSFORMATION POWER OF BEING HEARD

When people feel genuinely heard, walls come down. Teams move from surface-level conversations to deeper understanding. Ideas flow more freely, tensions ease, and solutions emerge more organically. Authentic listening transforms interactions from transactional to meaningful, laying the groundwork for deeper trust and shared success.

When listening is absent or insincere, conversations break down. People sense when you're simply waiting for your turn to speak, rather than truly understanding their perspective. When this happens, they pull back, trust erodes, and opportunities for growth and collaboration quietly slip away.

Just like a well-built bridge requires strong cables to carry its load, authentic listening is one of the most important cables in any relationship bridge. It bears the weight of understanding, empathy, and connection. With practice and genuine curiosity, we can turn listening from an overlooked habit into a daily superpower.

Empathy: Understanding Without Agreement

Empathy is the ability to understand and acknowledge the emotions and experiences of others. But more than that, it is the act of stepping into someone else's world and seeing things from their point of view. In every great team, empathy is the invisible thread that weaves people together, allowing them to connect, support, and collaborate at a deeper level.

THE NEUROSCIENCE OF CONNECTION

Neuroscience helps explain why empathy is so essential. Studies have shown that when we observe someone experiencing difficulty and imagine ourself in their position, the same regions of our brain activate as if we were experiencing it ourself. This demonstrates the neurological power of empathy. When we imagine another's experience, our brain reacts as though it is happening to us.

This is the heart of empathy, not just observing, but imagining. It is the mental act of moving from "I see you" to "I feel with you."

Research from the Center for Creative Leadership underscores this further. Leaders who consistently demonstrate empathy foster higher levels of employee engagement, innovation, and job satisfaction. Empathy is not just a "nice to have"; it is a competitive advantage. Teams that practice empathy solve problems more creatively, resolve conflicts more effectively, and support one another in ways that sustain performance over time.

EMPATHY IN REMOTE SETTINGS

Empathy becomes particularly crucial in hybrid and remote environments, because we miss many of the visual and contextual cues that help us understand what others are experiencing. When someone seems distracted or less engaged during a video call, empathy helps us consider that they might be dealing with childcare challenges, home-environment distractions, technology frustrations, or the unique stressors of remote work rather than immediately assuming disengagement or lack of commitment.

Effective remote leaders regularly check in about personal context and home situations, recognizing that the boundaries between work and personal life blur significantly when teams are distributed. They practice empathy by considering how different team members might be experiencing remote work differently based on their living situations, family responsibilities, and personal circumstances.

EMPATHY IN ACTION

Modeling empathy involves more than listening to someone's concerns. Empathy requires a genuine effort to see the situation through their eyes. It's the leader who pauses before jumping to conclusions about an underperforming employee, instead choosing to understand what pressures or challenges might be contributing. It's the coach who recognizes that a player struggling in practice might be carrying stress from personal life or school. It's the teammate who notices when someone seems overwhelmed and checks in, not to fix everything, but to say, "I see you."

One thing I always emphasize when I speak about empathy is this: Empathy does not require agreement. This is a crucial distinction. We can empathize with someone's feelings or experiences even if we see things differently. Empathy is about understanding, not necessarily endorsing.

This is where many leaders and teammates get stuck. They fear that by showing empathy, they are conceding a point. But empathy isn't about winning or losing; it's about connection. It's about creating enough emotional space for people to feel safe expressing themselves, even when their perspective differs from our own.

CREATING SAFE SPACES THROUGH EMPATHY

I've seen firsthand how empathy can shift a negative atmosphere. In environments where empathy is practiced, people engage more openly. Difficult conversations become easier because people trust that they will be heard, not judged. In families and personal relationships, empathy strengthens the bridge of connection, especially during challenging times when emotions run high.

When empathy is lacking, people begin to feel invisible or misunderstood. They withdraw. They stop sharing ideas and hold back contributions because they assume they won't be valued or respected. Over time, this weakens the very fabric of the team or relationship.

Just like a suspension bridge relies on strong cables to withstand pressure, teams depend on empathy to maintain connection and resilience. Empathy acts as the shock absorber during times of stress and keeps us steady in daily interactions. When people feel understood and supported, they invest more deeply in the relationship and in the goals of the team, strengthening the bridge that holds them together.

Specificity: Clear Expectations Drive Results

Specificity is the backbone of clarity in every relationship, team, or organization. It's the difference between vague hope and confident action. When we are specific about expectations, responsibilities, goals, and feedback, we remove ambiguity and build a foundation where accountability and trust can thrive.

WHY VAGUE COMMUNICATION FAILS

When expectations are vague, people fill in the blanks with their own assumptions. Unfortunately, those assumptions rarely align. What one person thinks is urgent, another assumes is optional. What one person believes is "good enough," another sees as falling short. Without specificity, cracks form in the bridge long before the weight of pressure arrives.

> When expectations are vague, people fill in the blanks with their own assumptions.

Research backs this up. Studies published in *Harvard Business Review* have shown that teams with clearly defined expectations and goals operate with greater efficiency, higher engagement, and stronger accountability. Conversely, teams plagued by vague communication often experience duplicated efforts, unmet deadlines, and a lack of ownership. It's not because people don't care; it's because they aren't clear on what's expected.

SPECIFICITY IN VIRTUAL ENVIRONMENTS

Without clear, explicit expectations, individuals working remotely or in hybrid settings can become uncertain about priorities, deadlines, and standards, leading to confusion, frustration, and decreased effectiveness. Virtual environments eliminate many of the informal check-ins and clarifying conversations that happen naturally in traditional office settings, making written and verbal specificity even more critical.

Effective virtual leaders become masters of specific communication: detailed project briefs, clear deadlines, explicit quality standards, and regular check-in protocols. They understand that what might be clarified in a quick hallway conversation must now be captured in clear, specific digital communication to ensure everyone stays aligned and accountable.

SPECIFICITY AS LEADERSHIP TOOL

Modeling specificity starts with the leader but belongs to everyone. It's the leader who sets clear objectives and ensures feedback is structured and actionable. It's the coach who breaks down the game plan so every player understands their role on the field. It's the teammate who doesn't assume others know what's expected but takes the time to confirm shared understanding. It's the family member who doesn't rely on unspoken rules but communicates openly about needs and responsibilities.

I often explain it this way: Specificity is decisiveness in action. When we are specific, we remove the guesswork. We create an environment where people can confidently move forward, knowing what success looks like and how their contribution fits into the bigger picture. This is especially important in moments of pressure, where clarity provides a stabilizing force amid uncertainty.

THE COST OF UNCLEAR EXPECTATIONS

Lack of specificity erodes trust just as much as broken commitments. When we're unclear, we leave people guessing. Tasks slip through the cracks. People hesitate to act because they're unsure of the priorities. Over time, frustration builds. Misunderstandings multiply. The bridge starts to weaken, not because people aren't trying, but because the structure wasn't sound to begin with.

Just like a suspension bridge relies on precisely placed cables to handle its load, strong teams depend on clearly defined expectations and structured accountability to stay stable under pressure. Each specific detail, from goals to roles to follow-through, adds strength and integrity to the bridge. The more precise we are, the more confidently our team can move forward together.

SPECIFIC RECOGNITION CREATES IMPACT

Specificity doesn't just apply to tasks and responsibilities. It applies equally to recognition and feedback. Vague praise like "great job" feels hollow. But when we tell someone exactly what they did well and why it mattered, the impact deepens. Specific feedback, whether positive or constructive, helps people grow and stay connected to the purpose of their work.

When specificity becomes part of the team's culture, collaboration strengthens. Misunderstandings decrease. People step up with clarity because they know exactly what's expected and how they contribute to the team's success.

How CABLES Work Together

These six behaviors aren't independent; they reinforce each other. Consistency makes your appreciation trustworthy. Belonging creates trust for honest listening. Empathy informs how you show specificity. When you practice all six regularly, you don't just build stronger relationships; you create an environment where others start practicing them too.

Working with teams across different industries, I've consistently seen that when these behaviors become part of the culture, everything changes. Trust deepens. Communication improves. Conflicts decrease. People engage more fully because they know their contributions matter and their relationships can handle the weight of honest feedback and shared challenges.

The teams that stand out don't just happen to have good chemistry. They've intentionally built it through these specific behaviors practiced consistently over time. They understand that strong relationships aren't accidents; they're engineered daily through the choices we make in how we show up for each other.

ASSESSING YOUR RELATIONSHIP BRIDGES

Strong relationships, whether among coworkers, teammates, family members, or partners, are built deliberately, not by default. Use the following bridge types to assess the strength of your connections. As you read each one, reflect on where your most important relationships stand today and what small actions could help them grow stronger.

FRAYED ROPE BRIDGE

A fragile connection marked by risk and hesitation.

This stage reflects relationships that are either new, neglected, or strained. There's little trust, limited communication, and high uncertainty. Whether it's a manager and direct report, a coach and player, a parent and teen, or partners after a tough season, each interaction feels uncertain. Inconsistency, unclear roles, and missed opportunities to connect keep this bridge unstable. It begins to strengthen through simple, repeated actions: showing up consistently, expressing interest, and recognizing effort honestly.

WORN CABLE BRIDGE

A connection with promise but still vulnerable under pressure.

At this stage, the relationship has some trust and familiarity, but the foundation hasn't been tested. There may be growing mutual respect or comfort, but stressors can still shake it. In a team setting, this might look like occasional collaboration without deeper cohesion. In a family or partnership, it may feel like coexistence without deeper emotional trust. Growth happens through intentional presence, specific appreciation, more meaningful conversations, and shared experiences that anchor trust.

STANDARD CABLE BRIDGE

A dependable connection but still with untapped potential.

This bridge can support everyday weight. Trust is reliable, communication is open, and minor conflicts have been worked through. However, assumptions and routine may keep the relationship from evolving. In the workplace, this may mean a team that functions but doesn't challenge each other to grow. In families or relationships, it might mean stability without depth. Advancing this bridge requires courage— courage to have hard conversations, offer thoughtful feedback, and align around shared values and goals.

RESILIENT CABLE BRIDGE

A strong, well-maintained connection that withstands adversity.

This relationship has weathered challenges and come out stronger. Communication is respectful and open, and there's a foundation of mutual trust. In any setting, this is the team, family, or partnership that rallies under stress and continues to support each other. But strength can invite complacency. To keep this bridge resilient, relationships must be continually nurtured: through celebrating past growth, anticipating future needs, and routinely resetting expectations together.

LEGACY CABLE BRIDGE

A high-trust, high-performance connection that endures and inspires.

This is more than a functioning relationship; it's a defining one. Whether in leadership, coaching, parenting, or partnership, this bridge stands on shared history, deep respect, and a sense of purpose. It performs under pressure and models what's possible for others. What sets it apart is the commitment to continual investment: showing up when it's inconvenient, growing together over time, and holding each other to the highest standards of care, honesty, and encouragement. This bridge isn't built quickly, but it lasts.

"Building Your Bridge" Action Plan

As you think about the relationships in your life, consider which ones feel like rope bridges in need of care and which are already reinforced and strong. Remember, no matter where your bridges are today, every one of them can be strengthened with small, consistent actions.

To help you assess the current strength of your relationship bridges more systematically, you can download a comprehensive CABLES assessment tool. This resource will help you evaluate your relationships across all six behaviors and identify specific areas for improvement with the key people in your professional and personal life.

The CABLES Behaviors are not complex, but they require intention. They don't demand perfection, but they do demand consistency. Start with one behavior. Choose one relationship that matters to you. Practice one CABLES Behavior for one week. Notice what changes—not just in the other person, but in yourself.

Strong bridges and strong teams aren't built through grand gestures or dramatic interventions. They're built through the daily choice to show up with Consistency, Appreciation, Belongingness, Listening, Empathy, and Specificity. When you make that choice consistently, you don't just improve your relationships. You model what's possible for everyone around you.

Key Takeaways

- Every relationship is a bridge strengthened through daily effort and care.
- Small, consistent behaviors build lasting strength, like strands woven into strong cables.
- Consistency builds trust by aligning words and actions, especially in hybrid environments where digital interactions become primary trust signals.
- Appreciation fuels motivation when it is meaningful, specific, and unexpected; virtual teams need more systematic recognition approaches.
- Belongingness requires intentional connection through proximity, frequency, duration, and positive intensity; virtual environments demand deliberate relationship-building efforts.
- Listening is your superpower; authentic listening creates space for trust and requires extra focus in virtual settings.
- Empathy deepens connection by imagining yourself in another's experience without requiring agreement; remote work contexts require additional empathy for home-environment factors.
- Specificity creates clarity, removing guesswork and empowering confident action; virtual teams especially need explicit, detailed communication to stay aligned.
- Every bridge can be strengthened with small daily actions, regardless of its starting point.
- The CABLES assessment tool provides a systematic way to evaluate and strengthen your most important relationships.

Reflection Questions

- Which CABLES Behavior do I consistently model well, and which needs the most attention?
- How might I increase the "positive intensity" of my interactions with key teammates, family members, or partner?
- What's one relationship bridge that would benefit from immediate strengthening, and which CABLES Behavior would have the biggest impact?
- When pressure or conflict arises, do I rely on the strength of my relationship bridges, or do I try to solve problems without considering the relational foundation?
- In hybrid or virtual settings, how am I adapting my CABLES Behaviors to create connection across digital channels?

Practice Prompt

Before moving on, choose one important relationship in your life. Download and complete the CABLES assessment tool to honestly evaluate the current strength of that bridge. Then pick one CABLES Behavior to focus on this week. Notice how small, consistent actions begin to add strength to your most important relationships.

In Chapter 5, we'll continue to expand on our master blueprint by learning what it takes to become a great teammate and why it is a vital component to building a great team.

PART TWO

BECOMING A
GREAT TEAMMATE

BLUEPRINT COMPONENT:
PROTECTING THE HEALTH OF WELLBEING OF THE BUILDERS

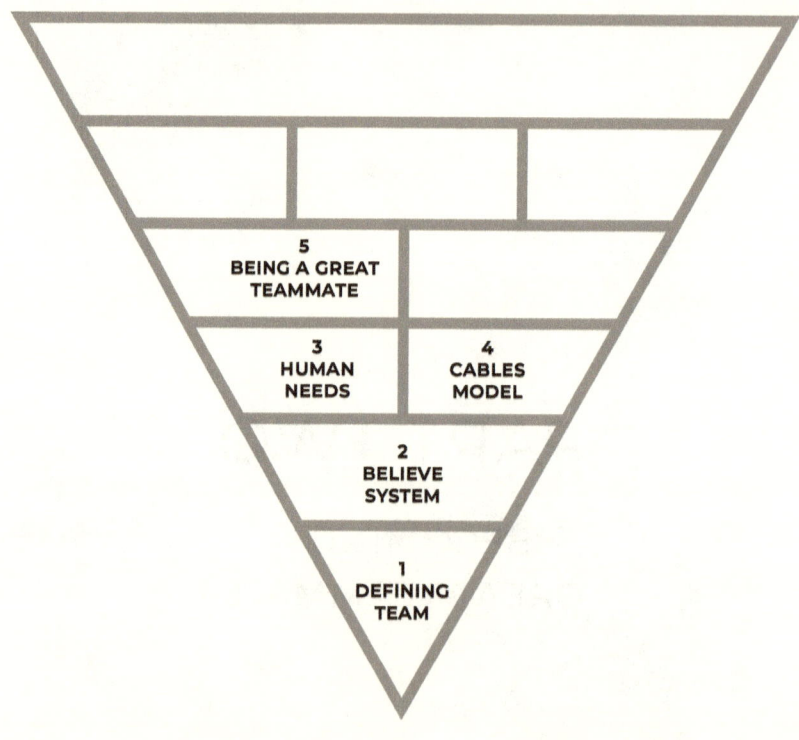

CHAPTER 5

GREAT TEAMS CAN ONLY EXIST WITH GREAT TEAMMATES

"The strength of the team is each individual member.
The strength of each member is the team."

– PHIL JACKSON

I've told all three of my children the same thing, whether they're heading into sports, school, work, or life: You cannot control whether you're placed on a great team, but you have complete control over whether you choose to be a great teammate. That choice is the only thing that gives you a real chance of being part of something great.

This advice isn't just for my kids. It's the foundation of every successful team I've studied. It is also what I emphasize when I present to teams and coach individuals. Great teams don't happen because talented people accidentally end up together. They happen because individuals decide to take responsibility for their own growth and contribution first.

But here's what most people miss: You can't consistently give what you don't have. Before you can support, celebrate, and challenge others authentically, you must first master these practices with yourself.

The Teammate Choice:
Personal Responsibility First

It may sound like a contradiction to say that great teammates put others first yet must care for themselves first. But both are true. You cannot give your best to someone else if you are running on empty. It is the same principle you hear before every commercial flight: In an emergency, put on your own oxygen mask before helping others. The point is simple. Without the capacity to breathe yourself, you cannot help anyone else breathe.

If you want to be part of a great team, you must first be committed to being a great teammate. That does not guarantee you will land on a great team, but failing to do it almost guarantees you will not. If you are not committed to being a great teammate, you risk becoming the reason the team cannot reach greatness.

The NEEDS Model and CABLES Behaviors we explored in the previous chapters create the foundation for healthy relationships and teams. But to consistently meet others' needs for connection, empowerment, equal treatment, dignity, and stability, you must first ensure your own foundation is strong. This isn't selfish; it's essential.

> If you are not committed to being a great teammate, you risk becoming the reason the team cannot reach greatness.

Why You Can't Give What You Don't Have

Being a great teammate is about how you treat others and how you treat yourself. The three pillars that define great teams (Support, Celebrate, and Challenge) must first be mastered personally before they can be offered authentically to others.

Self-support means having your own back. Self-celebration means honoring who you are and what you bring. Self-challenge means refusing to settle for less than the growth you are capable of. These do not exist in isolation. Just like in a team, challenge without support and celebration quickly turns into self-criticism, shame, or burnout. That is not growth; it is sabotage.

This is why I focus so much of my one-on-one work with leaders, athletes, coaches, parents, and partners on building strength in each of these areas personally. When you support, celebrate, and challenge yourself, you become a better teammate, a better leader, a better partner, and a better human being.

If you want to contribute more to your team, your workplace, your family, or your community, this is where it starts. Growth within yourself elevates everyone around you.

Support: Your Foundation for Giving

Support is often framed as something we give to others, but the truth is, you can't offer what you don't have. Being a great teammate begins with learning how to support yourself. It's about having your own back.

WHY SELF-SUPPORT ISN'T SELFISH

When you're physically depleted, mentally scattered, or emotionally burned out, you can't show up fully for anyone else. Whether you're leading a team, raising a family, coaching athletes, or navigating a relationship, your ability to positively influence others is directly tied to how well you take care of yourself.

The research is clear: Personal well-being fuels emotional regulation, increases resilience, and strengthens decision making. These are all critical for healthy relationships and effective leadership. Self-support isn't about putting yourself first; it's about ensuring you have something valuable to offer when others need you most. You may be wondering how you can go about building this resilience and personal well-being while experiencing challenging situations, which is why I have included a series of researched activities that improve personal well-being.

THE **POWER** JOURNAL FRAMEWORK

That's where the POWER (Praise, Others, Writing, Exercise, and Relaxation) Journal framework comes in. These five behaviors aren't fluff. They're evidence-based practices proven to improve emotional, psychological, and even physical well-being. And each one strengthens your foundation of support so you can better support those around you.

This is a model I have used for nearly a decade, and I fully believe in and have benefited from personally. It is a simple yet powerful tool that supports physical, emotional, intellectual, and spiritual well-being. I provide it to every participant in my leadership workshops as a resource they can continue to use on their own.

PRAISE: PRACTICE GRATITUDE

Gratitude is a mindset that rewires the brain for optimism, empathy, and perspective. Studies show that practicing gratitude consistently improves sleep quality, reduces aggression, and boosts self-esteem and resilience.

Application: Begin or end your day by naming three things you're grateful for, including something about yourself. This builds internal recognition and shifts your focus from what's missing to what's working.

OTHERS: PRACTICE GENEROSITY

Supporting yourself doesn't mean isolating from others; it means engaging in ways that energize rather than deplete. Acts of generosity, even small ones, activate areas of the brain linked to reward and connection. Research has found that helping others enhances purpose, decreases stress, and increases well-being for both the giver and the receiver.

Application: Do one intentional act of kindness each day—not for praise, but to remind yourself that you have something to offer. That's powerful reinforcement of self-worth. When working with leaders, I suggest that a way they can practice generosity is by thinking of someone they do not have a great relationship with and spending a few moments trying to connect with them in a more caring way. This is a demonstration that requires a deep investment in well-being for others.

WRITING: PROCESS THROUGH REFLECTION

Journaling has been shown to reduce stress, increase clarity, and improve emotional regulation. A foundational study by Emmons and McCullough found that individuals who wrote about things they were grateful for reported significantly higher levels of well-being than those who wrote about neutral or negative experiences.

Application: End each day with a few sentences about what went well or what you learned. This simple practice promotes emotional recovery and helps reframe challenges as growth moments.

EXERCISE: ENERGIZE YOUR MIND AND BODY

We often treat movement as optional, but the science doesn't support that thinking. A study published in *Psychosomatic Medicine* found that patients who exercised three times a week for thirty minutes experienced better outcomes for depression than those using medication alone, and the effect lasted months beyond the intervention.

Application: Schedule movement like you would a meeting. Even a short walk or stretching session improves mood, clarity, and stamina: tools every teammate needs.

RELAXATION: PRACTICE PRESENCE AND PEACE

Mindfulness-based stress reduction (MBSR) has been shown to improve focus, decrease anxiety, and reduce emotional reactivity. When you build mindfulness into your routine, you strengthen your ability to respond rather than react, which is an essential trait for any leader or teammate.

Application: Practice a brief breathing or grounding exercise daily. This exercise helps create clarity, awareness, and control over how you show up under pressure.

A LEADER'S PERSPECTIVE SHIFT

Recently a leader I had worked with contacted me to share his experience using the POWER Journal. He was facing serious challenges in his personal life and began using one of the exercises from the journal: writing down three things he was grateful for each morning. He had been doing this consistently for almost three months, and said it was making a real difference in how he approached his circumstances. The problems had not gone away, but his perspective had shifted.

This is exactly why self-support matters. When you gain that kind of perspective, you also show up better for the people around you. You can't lead others through difficulty if you haven't learned to navigate it yourself. That is the real benefit of this practice. Writing in the journal each morning will not eliminate your problems, but it can help you approach them with greater clarity and calm.

BUILDING YOUR SUPPORT NETWORK

Self-support isn't just about individual habits; it's also about building the relationships and systems that sustain you. This includes mentors who challenge your thinking, peers who understand your challenges, and routines that recharge your energy. Great teammates don't try to do everything alone.

We often talk about showing up for others, but if you're not investing in your own well-being, you're showing up depleted, reactive, or distracted. In leadership, parenting, coaching, and relationships, what you model matters. By prioritizing these practices, you're not just improving yourself; you're setting the standard for how others can support themselves too.

Your energy sets the emotional tone for the people around you. When you support yourself well, you become a steady, resilient presence others can rely on. That's what great teammates do. And it starts right here.

Celebrate: The Missing Piece of Growth

It would be easy to place "Celebrate" under the umbrella of self-support, and in some ways, it belongs there. But this pillar stands on its own for an important reason: Most of us don't struggle to push ourselves; we struggle to give ourselves credit.

WHY CELEBRATION MUST STAND ALONE

We're conditioned to overlook progress. We finish a hard day and focus on what didn't get done. We hit a milestone and immediately shift to what's next. While that drive can be useful, it can also be draining. Celebrate exists to keep that drive healthy. It gives us a moment to pause; not to settle, but to recognize what's already been accomplished. And that recognition builds the emotional momentum we need to keep going.

Celebration is different from support. Support is about maintenance and care. It's how we stabilize ourselves. But celebration is how we affirm ourselves. It's how we acknowledge effort, honor growth, and reinforce our own value, not because someone else said so, but because we see it for ourselves.

This matters, because when we skip celebration, we start believing we haven't done enough. That belief erodes confidence. It feeds comparison, burnout, and self-doubt. And it becomes a breeding ground for imposter syndrome, even in high performers. That's why this practice can't be optional; it has to be part of how we grow.

WHY YOUR BRAIN MISSES PROGRESS

When you intentionally recognize your own progress, you're not just being nice to yourself; you're literally rewiring your brain for resilience and motivation. The same dopamine pathways that respond to external recognition activate when you acknowledge your own growth. This isn't self-indulgence; it's neurological maintenance.

The problem isn't that we haven't accomplished anything; the problem is that we're not wired to notice it. The human brain has a built-in negativity bias, meaning we're more likely to remember what went wrong than what went well. It's a survival mechanism, but in everyday life, it distorts our self-perception.

You might have dozens of productive moments in a day, but one conflict, one mistake, or one unfinished task dominates your internal narrative. That's why you must be intentional about noticing and naming your progress. Celebration isn't about ignoring what needs work; it's about refusing to let that become the only thing you see.

CELEBRATE WITH CLARITY: NEUTRAL THINKING

Trevor Moawad's concept of neutral thinking helps reframe this. He taught that while the past is real, it's not predictive. Neutral thinkers don't ignore their mistakes, but they don't assign those mistakes permanent meaning either. They acknowledge the facts without judgment and focus on the next action.

When it comes to celebration, neutral thinking means you can say, "I didn't finish everything, but I kept showing up," or "That wasn't my best effort, but I learned from it." It frees you from self-pity and self-delusion. It lets you recognize effort without demanding perfection, and that recognition is where sustainable growth begins.

For example, imagine you set a goal to exercise five days this week but only made it three times. A neutral-thinking approach acknowledges the reality: "I exercised three times this week. That's three more than zero, and I showed up despite a packed schedule." Compare this to gap thinking: "I failed again. I can't even stick to a simple workout plan." One builds momentum; the other kills it. Or consider a manager who planned to have one-on-ones with all ten direct reports but only completed six. Neutral thinking says: "I connected with six people this week and learned valuable information about their projects. Next week, I'll prioritize the remaining four." This acknowledges the effort while maintaining forward focus.

From Gap to Gain: Reframing Success

In *The Gap and The Gain*, Dan Sullivan and Dr. Benjamin Hardy make this point even clearer: Stop measuring yourself against an ever-moving ideal (the gap), and start measuring against where you started (the gain). The gap mindset always leaves you feeling behind. But the gain mindset grounds you in reality. It acknowledges growth, even when you're still in progress.

This shift is essential. When you only see how far you have to go, you lose energy. But when you see how far you've come, you gain perspective, and that perspective fuels confidence.

Consider a sales professional who set a quarterly goal of closing twenty new accounts but closed fourteen. The gap mindset fixates on the missing six accounts and feels like failure. The gain mindset looks back to last quarter's eight accounts and recognizes seventy-five percent growth. Both perspectives are factually accurate, but only one builds the confidence to keep improving. Or think about a parent working on being more patient with their children. The gap mindset notices every moment they lost their temper. The gain mindset recognizes that they paused and took a breath before responding three times this week, when previously, they would have reacted immediately every time.

This is backed by *The Progress Principle*, which shows that recognizing even small wins has a significant impact on motivation, creativity, and overall well-being. The celebration doesn't have to be grand; it just has to be honest. A simple note of progress. A moment of reflection. A quick journal entry at the end of the day listing three things that went well. A team meeting that starts by acknowledging what got accomplished before diving into what's next. These acts reinforce your commitment to the process, and that's worth celebrating.

CHASING RABBITS: A RUNNER'S LESSON

As a competitive person, I've always been wired to chase the person ahead of me. I don't think there's anything wrong with that competition, as it often can drive growth. But there's a line we cross when we start using someone else's success as the measuring stick for our own worth. It is a line that took me many years to realize and still provides a challenge every so often.

When I started running road races, mostly 5Ks and 10Ks, I was pacing around eight minutes per mile. Over time, that dropped to about 6:10 pace per mile. But even as I improved, there was always someone faster. That's when I started picking runners ahead of me in a race that I could use as targets that I called "rabbits." If I caught one rabbit, I picked another. Sometimes I passed them. Sometimes I didn't. But I always got better.

The goal wasn't to beat them (half true); it was to stretch myself. This taught me something valuable about celebration and competition. Let others inspire you. Let them challenge you. But don't let them define you. You're not in their race. You're in yours. And as long as you're improving, you're winning.

This applies directly to teams and leadership. You can learn from others and even compete with them, but your worth isn't determined by where you rank. It's determined by whether you're growing, contributing, and becoming the teammate others can count on.

THE STOIC PATH TO SELF-RECOGNITION

I am a big fan of the Stoics and their teachings and observations. The Stoics understood the power of internal recognition long before modern psychology put language to it. Thinkers like Marcus Aurelius, Seneca, and Epictetus wrote not to impress others but to train themselves to reflect, refine, and realign their actions with their values.

One of the most influential resources I've come across in my own journey is *The Practicing Stoic* by Ward Farnsworth. I listen to it on Audible at least twice a year as a personal reset. I have found it to be grounding in its practical and relentlessly clear guidance from the Stoics. Farnsworth doesn't just explain Stoicism; he organizes it into a kind of philosophical user manual for life. It reminds me, every time I revisit it, that true strength comes not from control over outcomes, but from control over perception and response to those outcomes.

Stoic wisdom teaches us to focus on what we can control, observe our judgments without becoming them, and define success by integrity rather than applause. In today's terms, that's exactly what Celebrate asks of us. It's about honoring consistency over perfection. Effort over outcome. Principle over praise.

Celebration through a Stoic lens isn't self-congratulation; it's self-alignment. It's about living in a way you respect, regardless of who's watching. That kind of internal validation creates the confidence and resilience great teammates need.

Challenge: Rising Above Your Best

Challenge is often misunderstood. It's easy to think of it as pressure—as something external that forces us to stretch, hustle, or outperform. But in the context of becoming a great teammate, challenge isn't about competing against others or meeting someone else's standard. It's about raising the standard for yourself.

This pillar comes last for a reason. Without self-support, challenge becomes burnout. Without self-celebration, challenge becomes self-criticism. But when it's built on a foundation of self-care and fueled by acknowledgment of your growth, challenge becomes an invitation, not a demand. You're not trying to prove your worth. You're driven to expand your potential.

Real challenge isn't about perfection. It's about progress through difficulty.

Real challenge isn't about perfection. It's about progress through difficulty. It's about choosing discomfort when comfort would be easier. The goal isn't to constantly "grind"; it's to stay awake in your own life. To notice when you're coasting. To interrupt the narrative that says, "This is good enough," when you know it's not your best.

But challenge must come from a place of belief, not shame.

Self-challenge built on shame sounds like: "I'm not doing enough." "I'm not good enough." "I'll never be like them."

Self-challenge built on belief sounds like: "I know I'm capable of more." "I've made progress and I'm not done yet." "I'm not where I want to be, but I'm committed to getting there."

The difference is psychological and transformational. One drains you. The other drives you.

CHALLENGE STARTS WITH OWNERSHIP

You don't rise above your best through intention alone. You rise through ownership—the daily decision to act in ways that align with the person you're becoming. That includes the way you talk to yourself, how you respond to setbacks, how you use your time, and the effort you give when no one is watching.

High-performing teams, relationships, and families are built by individuals who take responsibility for their own growth. They don't wait to be pushed. They choose to push themselves. And that mindset is contagious.

You can't lead others where you aren't willing to go yourself.

One of the most deceptive barriers to growth is the idea we'll start when conditions are right, when we have more time, energy, support, or clarity. But personal growth doesn't wait for ideal circumstances. It happens because we act, despite the uncertainty.

The Stoics would call this preparation of the soul: training your character so that difficulty reveals your strength rather than your fear. In Farnsworth's *The Practicing Stoic*, that idea appears again and again. You don't hope for ease. You train for impact. That's the work of challenge.

To make challenge part of your life, you need a rhythm. One of the most effective ways to do this is through a weekly personal challenge check-in.

Ask yourself: Where did I play it safe this week? What discomfort did I choose and what did it teach me? What's one action I've been avoiding that I can lean into next?

Small, consistent challenges build compound strength. You don't need to upend your life. You just need to choose something each week that stretches your capacity.

Challenge is a mindset you train. Like exercise, it builds over time. You train it in the moments when you want to quit but don't. When you want to shrink but step up. When no one is watching and you still do the right thing.

That's what it means to "rise above your best"—not to be better than someone else, but to be better than who you were yesterday. To close the gap between your values and your actions. To become the kind of teammate, leader, parent, or partner others can count on, not because you're perfect, but because you're committed.

THE RIPPLE EFFECT OF PERSONAL GROWTH

When you consistently practice these three pillars, something interesting happens. Others start noticing. Your energy becomes more stable. Your confidence grows. Your responses to pressure improve. You become the kind of person others want to work with, learn from, and follow.

This isn't about perfection; it's about modeling what's possible when someone commits to continuous growth. You create the kind of presence that makes teams stronger simply by being part of them.

Research shows that leaders who invest in their own well-being are twenty-three percent more effective at managing stress, eighteen percent more resilient during setbacks, and significantly better at maintaining team morale during challenges. Personal development isn't separate from professional effectiveness; it's the foundation for it.

THE TEAMMATE OTHERS WANT TO FOLLOW

Great teams don't happen by accident, and they don't happen because of wishful thinking. They happen because individuals decide to take responsibility for their own growth, their own energy, and their own contribution to the culture around them.

When you support yourself, celebrate yourself, and challenge yourself consistently, you become someone others want to follow, work alongside, and learn from. You model what's possible when someone commits to continuous growth. You create the kind of presence that makes teams stronger simply by being part of them.

This isn't about perfection; it's about commitment and progress. Commitment to showing up as your best self, even when it's difficult. Commitment to growing when others are coasting. Commitment to being the kind of teammate you want to work with.

Remember what I told my children: You cannot control whether you're placed on a great team, but you have complete control over whether you choose to be a great teammate. That choice starts with how you treat yourself. It starts with taking responsibility for your own growth. It starts with becoming the person you want others to be.

Key Takeaways

- You can't consistently give what you don't have; personal development enables team contribution.
- Self-support through the POWER Journal framework builds the foundation for showing up fully for others.
- Self-celebration creates the motivation and resilience needed for sustained growth and contribution.
- Self-challenge pushes you beyond comfort zones and prevents plateau and complacency.
- The three pillars work together: Support enables challenge, Celebrate fuels motivation, Challenge drives growth.
- Personal growth creates ripple effects that transform every team and relationship you're part of.
- Great teammates take responsibility for their own development rather than waiting for others to create culture.

Reflection Questions

- How am I supporting myself through the habits that build physical, mental, and emotional resilience?
- Do I regularly recognize and celebrate my own progress, or do I only focus on what's left to accomplish?
- What areas of my life am I avoiding because they feel challenging or uncomfortable?
- How is my personal growth (or lack thereof) affecting the teams and relationships I'm part of?
- What would it look like to take complete ownership of my own development?
- If others modeled my approach to personal growth, would it create the kind of team culture I want to be part of?

Practice Prompt

Choose one of the three pillars (Support, Celebrate, or Challenge) and commit to focused development in that area for the next thirty days. Use the frameworks and practices outlined in this chapter, and document your progress. Notice how changes in your personal approach to growth begin to influence how you show up for others and how others respond to you.

What's Next

Understanding what great teams do and what great teammates contribute is only valuable if you can consistently implement these principles in your daily life and leadership. In Chapter 6, we'll explore how to turn all of these insights into sustainable action through practical frameworks that help you build great teams one relationship, one conversation, and one decision at a time.

The journey from good intentions to lasting change requires more than inspiration. It requires a system. And that's exactly what we'll build together next.

BLUEPRINT COMPONENT:
CONSTRUCTION AND PROJECT MANAGEMENT

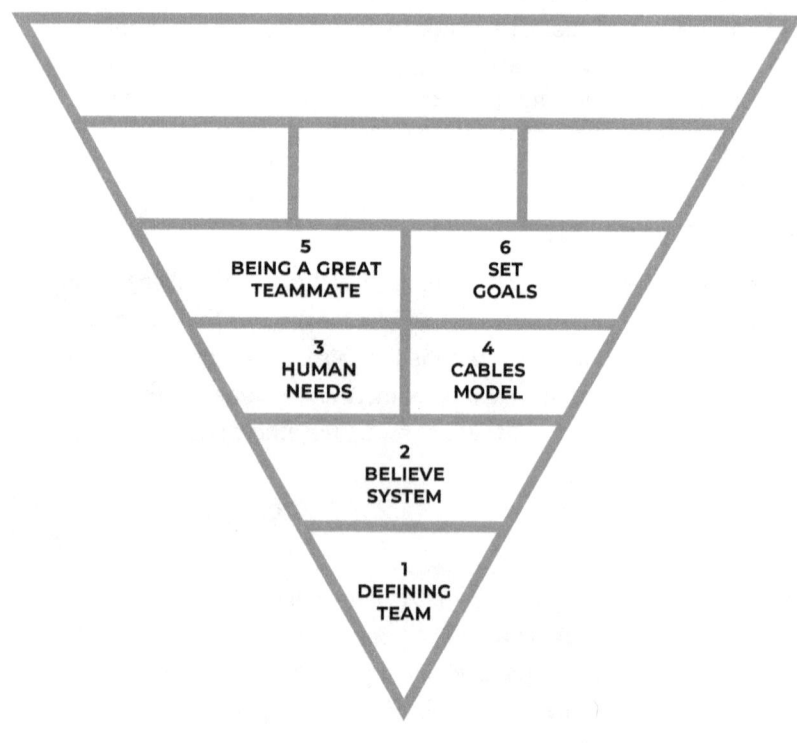

CHAPTER 6
ARE YOU SET FOR SUCCESS?

"The great danger for most of us is not that our aim is too high and we miss it, but that it is too low and we reach it."

– MICHELANGELO

You have now been introduced to what is involved in becoming a great teammate. You know how to support yourself, celebrate your progress, and challenge yourself to grow. Now comes the harder question: How do you turn that knowledge into lasting change? It's in goal achievement.

Most people don't struggle to set goals. They struggle to stay with them. That's where goal setting becomes essential, but not just any goal-setting approach.

Whether your goal is becoming a more supportive teammate, developing stronger leadership skills, building better relationships, or any meaningful personal change, success depends on building the habits and mindset to stay with it when motivation fades.

Why Many Struggle With Goals

Some goals are milestone goals. These are clear accomplishments with a defined endpoint—things like earning a promotion, hitting a revenue target, or completing a certification. They matter, but once the milestone is reached, the goal is complete.

Other goals are process goals. These are ongoing commitments to show up differently. Running three times a week. Listening more attentively. Being more present with others. These goals don't end with a single result. They represent a new way of living and leading.

The SET Model applies to both. Because no matter the type of goal, success depends on building the habits and mindset to stay with it when motivation fades.

The Pattern I Kept Seeing in Coaching

For years, I used the SMART goal model: Specific, Measurable, Achievable, Relevant, and Time-bound. It made sense on paper. But in practice, something was missing.

SMART goals provided clarity but not commitment. They outlined what to do but not the fuel to keep doing it, especially when things got hard.

Over time, I noticed a familiar pattern. Strong starts were followed by stalled progress. People were clear on their goals but struggled to stay connected to them. Motivation faded. Momentum disappeared. Frustration took its place.

A Coach's Profound Challenge That Changed Everything

My own breakthrough in understanding this came through working with my own coach. I had developed a habit that was sabotaging my progress, and I didn't even realize it. Whenever I hadn't completed something we had discussed in our previous session, I would start our next meeting by explaining that I "didn't have time" to do it.

After the second time this happened, my coach made me start saying something different. Instead of "I didn't have time," he made me say, "I chose not to make the time to do what I said I would do."

That simple change in language had a profound impact on how I approached commitments. It forced me to own the reality that if something was important enough to commit to, then I would find the time to do it. The issue wasn't time; it was priority and systems.

This experience taught me that goal achievement isn't about time management or willpower. It's about building the right relationship with your commitments and having systems that support follow-through.

That led me to a deeper question: What actually drives goal achievement, not just goal setting?

What Separates Those Who Follow Through

When I studied people who followed through consistently, across many areas of life, a clear pattern emerged. They didn't just set goals. They built a relationship with them.

They had a clear and meaningful outcome, a defined timeline, an emotional reason to care, gratitude for every step forward, a belief that success was possible, and the grit to keep going when it wasn't easy.

These elements went beyond what the SMART framework offered, which is why I created the SET Model: a framework designed not only for setting goals but for following through on them. SET provides the structure, while GET builds the mindset and habits needed for consistent execution.

Whether your goal involves personal growth, stronger leadership, better relationships, or any meaningful change, this model helps close the gap between intention and action. Setting a goal is easy. Following through is what actually drives transformation.

Understanding the SET Model

If goal setting alone were enough, most of us would already be where we want to be.

We don't fall short because we lack desire. We fall short because we lack a system that supports sustained progress. We often don't need more motivation. We need a map we can follow and the mindset to keep going when the path gets hard.

That's what the SET Model is designed to provide.

Unlike other models that stop at the planning stage, SET helps you move from inspiration to execution. It combines two essential components:

SET: How to define your goal with clarity and urgency.

- **Specific:** clearly defined and actionable.
- **Emotional:** tied to a purpose that fuels commitment.
- **Time-bound:** grounded in a realistic but motivating timeline.

The SET Framework:
Establishing the Right Goals

SPECIFIC: DEFINING THE GOAL CLEARLY

If you can't clearly define what success looks like, don't be surprised when people don't achieve it, including yourself.

The first ingredient of a strong goal is specificity. When a goal is vague, it invites misalignment. People interpret it differently. Execution becomes inconsistent. Specificity changes that. It provides the clarity teams, families, and relationships need to move forward together.

Psychologists Edwin Locke and Gary Latham spent decades studying goal setting and found that specific goals consistently lead to higher performance than general ones. When a goal is clearly defined, your brain starts scanning for ways to align behavior to that outcome. It's similar to setting a GPS destination. Without specificity, it's like typing "somewhere nice" into the search bar and hoping you arrive where you want to be.

I believe that when goals are truly specific, they become inherently measurable, which eliminates the need for the "M" in the traditional SMART model. True specificity already answers the question of how you'll know when you've achieved it. The measurement is built into the clarity.

"Improve communication" is not a specific goal. "Each team member will provide constructive feedback in our Thursday meeting for the next eight weeks" is. Notice how the specificity automatically creates the measure: you can count whether feedback happened in those meetings.

"Be a better parent" is too vague to act on. "Spend twenty distraction-free minutes with each child twice a week doing an activity of their choice" creates both structure and opportunity, and you can easily track whether those minutes happened.

"Connect more as a couple" sounds good but probably won't stick. "We'll commit to two technology-free meals a week to talk about something other than logistics" is clear, inherently measurable through those two meals, and doable.

Specific goals help people focus and reduce friction. When teams aren't specific, people default to assumptions, and effort gets scattered.

To create a specific goal, ask:

- What exactly do we want to achieve?
- Who is responsible?
- What does success look like in behavior, not just intention?
- How will we know we've accomplished it?
- Specificity doesn't make a goal harder. It makes it possible.

EMOTIONAL: CONNECTING TO A STRONG WHY

A clear goal can give you direction. An emotionally connected goal gives you staying power.

There's a reason the second Friday in January has earned the nickname "Quitter's Day." It's when most New Year's resolutions die. Gyms empty out. Meal-prep containers gather dust. Ambitious projects get quietly abandoned. The initial enthusiasm that felt so strong on January 1 has evaporated by midmonth, and people give up. Why? Because most goals, including the popular SMART framework, miss the most critical element: a strong why. Without emotional connection, goals become obligations we endure rather than commitments we embrace.

> A clear goal can give you direction. An emotionally connected goal gives you staying power.

In every field I've worked, I've seen the same thing: Goals that lack emotional connection rarely survive the first real obstacle. When the work gets hard, when energy dips, or when results are slow, people abandon goals they don't feel connected to. They hit Quitter's Day, whether it's in January or any other moment when motivation wanes, and they walk away.

Emotion is the fuel that sustains effort. Self-determination theory shows that long-term motivation depends on intrinsic motivation—when individuals feel a sense of autonomy, purpose, and emotional investment in what they're doing.

In *The Talent Code*, Dan Coyle studied people who had reached extraordinary levels of success. Whether they were Olympians, musicians, or world-class performers, they all shared a common starting point: an internal ignition. Something had sparked them from within. They weren't just chasing outcomes; they were pulled forward by a sense of purpose that made the goal personal. This emotional connection is what carried them through the inevitable Quitter's Days they faced along their journey.

When people understand why a goal matters and it connects to something that feels personal, they are more likely to stay engaged through difficulty and setbacks.

Let's say a team sets a goal to increase revenue by ten percent. That sounds clear but without emotional connection, it risks becoming a hollow number. Now imagine that same team connects the goal to something deeper: "We're growing revenue so we can avoid layoffs, expand benefits, and create more opportunity for our families and community." That version has heart. It matters. When the second Friday rolls around and motivation dips, that emotional connection becomes the difference between pushing through and giving up.

People don't abandon goals because they're too hard. They abandon them because they stop feeling worth the effort.

THE FIVE WHYS FOR STRENGTHENING BUY-IN

One of the simplest tools for identifying emotional connection is the Five Whys. When you state a goal, ask "Why?" five times in a row, each time drilling deeper into what truly matters.

For example: Goal: "I want to exercise more." → Why? "To feel healthier." → Why? "So I have more energy." → Why? "Because I want to be more present with my kids." → Why? "Because I've noticed I'm tired and distracted around them." → Why? "Because I don't want to miss these years; I want them to remember I was engaged."

Now it's no longer about exercise. It's about presence. That kind of goal is harder to walk away from when motivation fades.

You can apply this immediately by asking yourself or your team:

- Why does this goal matter to me or to us?
- What is at stake if we achieve it?
- What is at stake if we don't?
- How will this impact the people I care about?

People don't abandon goals because they're too hard. They abandon them because they stop feeling worth the effort.

TIME-BOUND: CREATING URGENCY AND STRUCTURE

A goal without a time frame is just a wish. It might feel important, but without a deadline or frequency, it won't feel urgent.

Our brains respond best to urgency. When we set a deadline, a rhythm, or a time-based commitment, it moves a goal from abstract to actionable. Parkinson's Law states that "work expands so as to fill the time available for its completion." When no deadline exists, most people will unconsciously delay taking action, even on things they say matter.

A leader who says "Let's improve engagement" may have good intent but no direction. A better frame: "By the end of the quarter, we'll conduct two pulse surveys and hold three listening sessions to address what's most important."

A parent might say, "I want to spend more time with my kids." But a time-bound version, "Every Sunday, 1–3 p.m., is our no-phone family time," turns the idea into a new habit.

Time-bound goals help us avoid the trap of perpetual planning. They also reduce overwhelm. Big goals often feel heavy because we don't know where to start. But breaking them into smaller time-based steps makes progress visible and repeatable.

There's a hidden benefit too: consistency over time builds identity. When someone consistently shows up for a goal, even in small ways, they begin to see themselves differently—not just "trying to lead," but becoming a dependable leader.

As you revisit your goals, ask:

- What is the start date and end date?
- How frequently will this be done?
- How will we track progress along the way?

Great teams are built on ownership, not obligation—and by shifting from SMART to SET, you move goal setting from a task people complete to a commitment they care about, which is the foundation of a culture where accountability happens naturally.

SMART vs. SET: Why SET Creates Ownership, Not Just Compliance

Dimension	SMART Model	SET Mode	Why SET Wins
Structure	Five-step process: Specific, Measurable, Achievable, Realistic, Time-bound	Three-step process: Specific, Emotional, Time-bound	Simpler and faster to apply, easier to remember and use consistently
Motivation	Largely cognitive and task-focused	Anchored in emotion and purpose	Emotional connection sustains action long after initial enthusiasm fades
Behavioral Outcome	Encourages compliance ("I have to")	Inspires ownership ("I want to")	Ownership drives discretionary effort, resilience, and follow-through
Engagement	Often transactional, goals feel like checklists	Deeply personal, goals feel meaningful	Meaning drives persistence when challenges arise
Cultural Impact	Builds accountability, people meet expectations	Builds commitment, people exceed expectations	Commitment is the foundation of great teams and sustained results

Bottom line: SMART goals help people plan. SET goals help people commit. And ownership, not accountability, is what transforms individual effort into lasting achievement.

Staying Energized and Dialed In:
Three Ways to Achieve Your SET Goals

With Specific, Emotional, and Time-bound in place, you've built a strong foundation for your goal. You know exactly where you're going, why it matters, and when you intend to get there. But setting a goal is only the beginning. The real question is: How do you sustain the energy and focus needed to see it through?

Most people abandon their goals not because they lack ability, but because they lose momentum somewhere between the starting line and the finish. The excitement fades. Progress feels slow. Obstacles show up. And without a way to stay energized and connected to the goal, they drift away from what they said mattered most.

The good news? You don't need superhuman willpower or perfect circumstances. You need three simple practices that keep you grounded, focused, and moving forward, especially when motivation wanes. Think of these as the fuel that powers your journey from intention to achievement.

1. RECOGNIZE PROGRESS ALONG THE WAY

Most people abandon their goals not because they're lazy, but because they lose sight of progress. When you focus only on what hasn't been done or how far you still have to go, it's easy to become discouraged. But when you intentionally acknowledge what has been accomplished, you build the emotional resilience to keep moving forward.

This is about shifting your focus from what's missing to what's working. Research from the University of Pennsylvania found that individuals who regularly practiced this kind of recognition reported higher levels of optimism, motivation, and perseverance, all critical to sustained goal pursuit. Almost all high-level athletes, effective leaders, resilient families, and strong partners share one behavior in common: they notice effort. They acknowledge growth. They celebrate small wins as well as learning and persistence.

Think of your goal like a long-distance journey on a winding road. You might not see the destination yet, but recognizing progress is the mile marker that reminds you you're still moving forward. It doesn't change the distance ahead. It changes your relationship to the road. The people and teams who notice those mile markers are the ones who don't turn back when the weather changes or the path gets steep. They keep going because they know they're already on the way.

Here's how it plays out in different roles:

A leader who opens weekly meetings by acknowledging progress creates a culture of momentum and motivation.

A coach who recognizes an athlete's improvement, not just their performance, reinforces behaviors that lead to long-term growth.

A parent who says, "I saw how hard you worked this week, even when you were frustrated," teaches their child to value effort, not just results.

A partner who notices and expresses appreciation for daily contributions builds trust and emotional trust.

Make it practical. Build recognition into your routine. Start meetings by naming one small win. Create a habit of journaling one thing you're grateful for in your goal journey. Catch someone doing something right and name it. Reflect weekly: What moved us closer this week, even if it wasn't perfect?

Try this three-minute practice:

- Write down three specific signs of progress you've made toward your goal in the past seven days.
- Write down who else contributed to that progress, even in a small way, and consider recognizing them.
- Ask yourself: "What's one thing I can appreciate about where I am right now, even if I'm not where I want to be yet?"

This simple practice builds awareness, perspective, and connection while training your mind to recognize progress before it slips by unnoticed.

2. BELIEVE IN SUCCESS BEFORE IT HAPPENS

Before any achievement becomes real, it has to be believable, not just in theory, but in your gut. This is the internal belief that success is possible and worth pursuing. When you expect a goal to happen, you begin acting in ways that make it more likely to happen. The mindset comes first. The behavior follows.

Research shows that people are more likely to engage in a task when they believe their effort will lead to meaningful results. Brain-imaging studies show that visualizing success activates the same neural pathways used when we actually perform the task. Belief and behavior are biologically connected.

You've likely seen this already:

A leader who expresses confidence in their team's ability to solve a tough problem changes the team's posture from hesitant to proactive.

A coach who consistently tells a player, "You've got what it takes," helps them play with presence instead of pressure.

A parent who reinforces effort and belief ("You've done hard things before. I know you can handle this one.") builds a child's internal voice.

This belief is contagious. When someone you respect believes in you, it makes it easier to believe in yourself. Think of it like a runway light in dense fog. Even when you can't clearly see the destination, belief gives you just enough visibility to keep moving forward. It doesn't promise there won't be turbulence. But it helps you trust the landing is possible, so you stay in motion.

Consider Leicester City Football Club in 2015. They were expected to fight just to survive relegation from the English Premier League. The odds of them winning the league? 5,000 to 1, the same odds some bookmakers gave for Elvis still being alive. And yet, they didn't just survive, they won the entire Premier League title.

What changed? Not talent. Not money. It was believing. Led by manager Claudio Ranieri, the players adopted a mindset of daily effort and unwavering belief. They blocked out the noise, focused on progress, and repeated a simple internal mantra: "Why not us?" Players like Jamie Vardy and Wes Morgan later reflected that it wasn't skill alone; it was the team's belief in each other that made the impossible possible. They started playing like a team that expected to win before the rest of the world believed it was possible. That's what belief does. It transforms effort from tentative to committed.

The counterbalance: While believing in success helps you see the runway, ancient wisdom offers a complementary strategy: imagine the consequences of not following through. The Stoics called this *premeditatio malorum*, mentally rehearsing what could go wrong if you don't act. It wasn't meant to create fear, but to sharpen focus.

Sometimes believing in success means being honest about the cost of taking the easy path. If you stop showing up, what gets lost? If you give in to distraction, what happens to the people counting on you? What's the real consequence of quitting? Together, belief in success and awareness of consequences create a resilient mindset: hopeful and prepared.

3. DO THE WORK, ESPECIALLY WHEN IT'S HARD

Recognition keeps you grounded. Belief keeps you focused. But consistent action is what keeps you going. It's the simplest and hardest part of achieving your goals. Because sustained action is not about dramatic effort. It's about deliberate consistency.

If you want a result, you need repetition. If you want transformation, you need to keep showing up. Psychologist Angela Duckworth defines grit as "passion and sustained persistence toward long-term goals." Her research shows that what separates top performers isn't just talent; it's their willingness to keep showing up long after the excitement has faded.

This isn't about inspiration. It's about implementation. The best leaders, partners, parents, and performers don't decide what to do based on how they feel. They've built the discipline to act, even when they'd rather not.

This mindset shows up everywhere:

A leader who holds one-on-one check-ins, even when their calendar is packed, builds trust that endures.

A coach who insists on daily fundamentals, win or lose, develops athletes who are resilient, not just skilled.

A parent who keeps reinforcing values through emotional fatigue creates trust and growth.

A partner who shows up for the relationship during hard seasons builds love that lasts.

Think of it like putting in the reps at the gym. Each individual rep doesn't feel heroic. Most don't feel inspiring. But over time, they change who you are if you stay consistent. People often say, "I just need to get motivated." But real motivation usually shows up after the reps, not before.

Few athletes modeled this the way Kobe Bryant did. It wasn't just his talent that stood out; it was his approach to work. One story from the 2008 Olympics says it all. Team USA's strength coach got a call from Kobe at 4:15 a.m., asking if he could meet him at the gym. By the time the coach arrived, Kobe was already deep into his workout. This wasn't before a game; it was before the team's scheduled practice later that day, which Kobe participated in fully, then returned again for more individual reps afterward. This wasn't about proving a point. It was his routine. He once said, "Great things come from hard work and perseverance. No excuses."

The public saw the championships. What they didn't see were the early mornings, the drills, and the years of repetition. That's what built his foundation. Consistency isn't about intensity every once in a while. It's about showing up over time.

This is where lead measures become crucial. Lead measures are the specific actions that influence outcomes, the reps you can control. If your goal is to improve client retention, the lead measure might be five proactive check-ins each week. If your goal is to strengthen your relationship, the lead measure might be two technology-free meals each week together. These are the things you can control and track.

When you pair structure with consistency, you stop guessing whether you're making progress and you can see it. And that clarity makes it easier to keep going.

Try this: Ask yourself:

- What's one small action that will move me closer to my goal this week?
- When will I do it?
- How will I make sure it happens on the day I don't feel like it?

Now take that action. Then take it again tomorrow. That's how goals become reality.

Overcoming Common Roadblocks

Even with a strong goal and the right practices, the path to achievement is rarely smooth. Obstacles show up. Motivation dips. Life gets in the way. This isn't a sign that the goal is wrong. It's a sign that you're doing something that matters. The key is not to avoid the roadblocks; it's to know how to navigate them.

When motivation fades: Use recognition to reset perspective. Ask: "What progress have I made that I might be overlooking? What did I show up for this week that would have been easy to skip? Who has helped me along the way?" Recognition reminds you that you're not starting over. You're continuing forward.

When doubt creeps in: Strengthen your belief with vision and evidence. Ask: "What's the best version of this outcome I can visualize right now? When have I done something difficult before and how did I pull it off? Who around me believes in this goal and how can I borrow their belief today?" Doubt will visit. But if belief answers the door, it doesn't get to stay.

When progress slows: Focus on repeatable action and consistency. Ask: "What's one thing I can keep doing, even in a low-energy week? What's the minimum baseline action that keeps me engaged? How can I stay accountable without relying on motivation?" The best don't succeed because they avoid slowdowns. They succeed because they keep moving anyway.

WHEN YOU KNOW WHAT'S COMING, YOU DON'T GET STUCK

The roadblocks you'll face aren't unusual. In fact, they're predictable. And that's what makes them manageable. When motivation dips, recognizing progress grounds you. When doubt creeps in, belief lifts you. When progress slows, consistent action carries you forward. These moments aren't detours. They're part of the path. How you respond will determine where you end up.

From Insight to Implementation

The SET framework isn't just another goal-setting method; it's a complete system for turning intention into achievement. Whether you're building stronger habits as a teammate, developing leadership skills, improving relationships, or pursuing any meaningful personal growth, this framework provides both the structure and the practices you need to follow through.

What makes SET different is its integration of planning and execution, and its alignment with the personal-development principles we explored in Chapter 5. SET gives you clarity and direction. These three practices give you the daily habits and mental patterns that sustain progress when motivation fades and obstacles appear.

Now that you understand how to support, celebrate, and challenge yourself personally, and have a framework for achieving meaningful goals, we turn to how these same principles create extraordinary teams. In the chapters that follow, we'll explore the three pillars that define what great teams actually do: Support, Celebrate, and Challenge.

These aren't just nice concepts; they're the behavioral foundations that transform ordinary groups into high-performing teams. And they begin with Support, the cornerstone that makes everything else possible.

Key Takeaways

- Goal-setting alone isn't enough; execution systems determine whether goals become reality.
- SET provides the structure: Specific goals eliminate confusion, Emotional connection fuels persistence, Time-bound deadlines create urgency.
- Gratitude maintains perspective, Expectancy builds belief, Tenacity sustains action.
- The framework builds on personal Support, Celebrate, and Challenge principles.
- Roadblocks are predictable and manageable when you have specific strategies.
- Personal accountability starts with honest language about choices, not circumstances.

Reflection Questions

- What goals have I set but failed to achieve, and where did the breakdown occur in SET?
- How can I make my current goals more specific, emotionally connected, and time-bound?
- What gratitude, expectancy, and tenacity practices will I build in to my routine?
- How can I apply SET to help my team, family, or organization achieve shared objectives?

Practice Prompt

Choose one meaningful goal and apply the complete SET framework. Write it using the SET criteria, then establish daily practices to support it. Use the roadblock strategies when challenges arise. Track your progress for thirty days and notice how the framework changes both your approach and your results.

Looking Ahead:
The Foundation of All Great Teams

Personal development creates the capacity to contribute meaningfully to others. But when groups of committed individuals come together, something even more powerful becomes possible. Chapter 7 will uncover the first pillar that separates great teams from merely functional ones: Support.

You'll discover why psychological trust isn't just a buzzword but the foundation that enables everything else. We'll examine how leaders, coaches, parents, and partners use specific CABLES Behaviors to create environments where people feel secure enough to take risks, share ideas, and give their absolute best. Because when people know others truly have their back, they're willing to go further than they ever thought possible.

Great teams don't happen by accident. They're built by individuals who've done the personal work and then commit to having each other's backs. That's where we're headed next.

PART THREE

BECOMING A GREAT TEAM

BLUEPRINT COMPONENT:

HOW TO BUILD THE SUPPORT TOWER

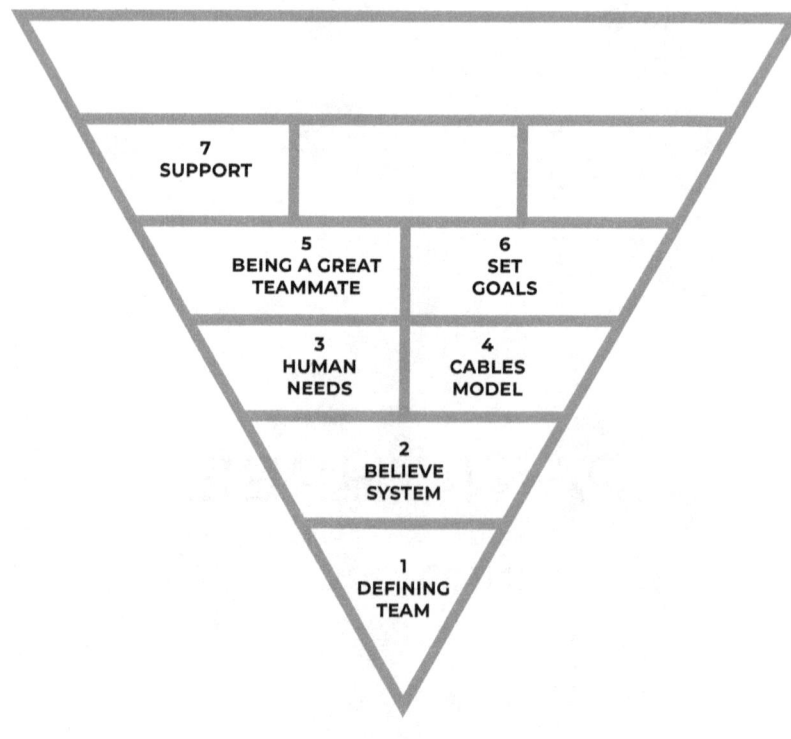

CHAPTER 7
WHY SUPPORT COMES FIRST

*"People don't care how much you know
until they know how much you care."*

– THEODORE ROOSEVELT

One recent morning, while writing this book, Cyndi stepped into my office and asked if I wanted to share a cup of coffee and sit on the porch. I was deep in a chapter, deadline pressure mounting, thoughts scattered across multiple documents. The easy answer would have been, "Maybe later," or "Let me just finish this section." But I paused, looked up, and said yes.

We spent fifteen quiet minutes together sipping coffee and tossing peanuts to the crows she'd somehow managed to befriend. We didn't solve any problems. We didn't have any profound conversations. We just sat together, present in the moment, supporting each other by choosing connection over the endless list of things that could wait.

It was a small moment. But it mattered.

That's what support actually looks like. Not grand gestures or dramatic interventions, but small, consistent choices that say "I'm here for you." In a world obsessed with productivity and achievement, we often miss the truth that great teams aren't built on talent alone. They're built on the deep trust that comes from knowing others will show up when it matters.

Support isn't the soft skill that gets attention. It's the foundational behavior that makes everything else possible. And while I've opened with a personal example from my marriage, these are the exact same behaviors that make organizational and sports teams great. The context changes, but the principle remains: People perform best when they know someone has their back.

If you've read and applied the previous chapters, you're now ready to understand just how powerful this pillar truly is.

Look at what you've already built. You've laid the foundation by understanding what drives human engagement through the NEEDS Model. You've added the connecting CABLES Behaviors that strengthen every relationship. You've discovered what it means to become a great teammate and learned how to turn meaningful goals into consistent action through SET.

These aren't just concepts you read about. They're the essential building materials on your master blueprint for creating a great team. And your reading and application of those previous chapters has now laid the foundation strong enough to build the first pillar: Support.

This is where everything shifts. This is where a collection of individuals starts becoming something more powerful than the sum of their parts. But here's what most people miss: The order matters. You can't skip ahead. You can't start with the flashy stuff. Great teams aren't built on talent or strategy alone. They're built on a sequence of behaviors that must happen in exactly the right order.

The three pillars—Support, Celebrate, and Challenge—represent what great teams actually do differently. Each one builds the foundation for the next. Try to challenge before you support, and people shut down. Try to celebrate before you've created trust, and it feels hollow. But get the sequence right, and something remarkable happens. People start taking ownership. They stop waiting to be told what to do and start seeing problems as their responsibility to solve. They have each other's backs not because they're supposed to, but because they want to.

And it all starts here, with Support.

This isn't about lowering standards or avoiding difficult conversations. It's about creating the psychological trust that allows people to take risks, share ideas, and give their best effort without fear. It's about building the kind of trust that makes everything else possible. Without this pillar, the other two can't stand. But with it? You create the conditions where ordinary teams become extraordinary.

What Cyndi and I shared that morning on the porch, that's the essence of what we're building here. Simple, intentional, consistent support that says "We are here for each other." Whether it's a marriage, a sales team, a coaching staff, or a project group, that's where great teams begin.

The Pace Principle

Great teams understand something that average teams miss: moving together doesn't mean moving at the same speed all the time. It means staying connected while pushing toward the same destination.

I've seen this play out countless times in both business and sports. Sometimes one team member is flying, operating at peak performance, hitting every milestone. Other times, that same person is struggling, overwhelmed, or simply hitting a wall. Meanwhile, their teammates might be in completely different places.

Here's what separates great teams from average ones: Great teams adjust their pace to stay connected—not to slow down permanently, but to regroup and then push further together than anyone could alone.

This is not about lowering standards. It's the opposite. Think of a cycling team in the Tour de France. When a lead rider faces a mechanical issue or exhaustion, the team doesn't abandon them or demand they keep pace. They slow down, regroup, and once everyone is back together, they push harder as a unit. That temporary adjustment creates the conditions for the entire team to go farther and faster than any individual could manage alone.

In business, this might look like a project manager noticing a team member drowning in work and redistributing tasks so everyone can push toward the deadline together. In sports, it's the star player who stays after practice to work with a struggling teammate, knowing that lifting everyone's performance strengthens the entire team.

In hybrid and remote environments, this becomes even more critical. Distance naturally creates different speeds and rhythms. Effective virtual leaders actively monitor team pace through regular touchpoints, transparent progress tracking, and buddy systems where team members check in with each other regularly. What used to happen naturally through physical proximity must now be deliberately designed into team rhythms.

But the principle remains the same: We adjust our pace not to lower our standards, but to ensure we can push further together.

At the heart of every great team—whether in business, sports, family, or anywhere people rely on each other—is one simple truth: they have each other's backs. No matter how talented a team might be, if people don't feel that those around them will step up when it matters, they pull back. They hesitate. They protect themselves instead of each other, and what could be a strong team becomes a weak one.

What "Having Their Back" Really Means

When I talk about support, I define it simply: having each other's backs. I often ask people to think about someone they've worked with who always had their back. Then I ask, "If that person came to you needing help, even on your busiest day, would you turn them away?" No one ever says yes. That's the power of building an environment where people genuinely feel supported. When people know you've got their back, they'll go out of their way to have yours. Support builds trust, and trust builds reciprocity.

There's an old story, told in many cultures, about a man who asked to see the difference between Heaven and Hell. In both places, he saw a table piled high with food and people holding spoons with handles so long they could not feed themselves. In Hell, people were starving because they only tried to feed themselves. In Heaven, people were healthy and content because they fed each other.

Great teams work like that second table. They understand that the fastest way to build a thriving environment is to focus on others first. When you act with the intention of helping those around you succeed, you create a culture of mutual investment where everyone benefits.

The Research Behind Support

This truth isn't just a moral lesson. It's backed by some of the most comprehensive research on human flourishing ever conducted. *The Good Life*, based on the Harvard Study of Adult Development spanning more than eighty years, reveals that strong relationships are the single strongest predictor of life satisfaction and well-being. But the research goes deeper: It's not just having relationships that matters, it's taking a genuine interest in others that builds the deepest bonds.

When we show sincere care for what matters to the people around us, such as their challenges, growth, and daily experiences, we create the trust and psychological trust that turns ordinary groups into extraordinary teams.

Support isn't just a good intention or a convenient offer of help; it's an everyday behavior. It shows up in how we work, how we communicate, and how we treat each other when things are going well and, more importantly, when they aren't.

How Support Meets Core Needs

Support ensures that others' core NEEDS are met. It fosters connection, empowers people to contribute, reinforces equal treatment, upholds dignity, and provides the stability that teams rely on. When support is missing, people protect themselves instead of trusting others.

> Support isn't just a good intention or a convenient offer of help; it's an everyday behavior.

But knowing that support is important isn't enough. Leaders, parents, coaches, and teammates need to know how to put support into action. That's where the CABLES Model comes in. If the NEEDS Model explains why support is essential, CABLES shows us how to build it.

While all six behaviors in the CABLES Model contribute to stronger relationships, it's Consistency, Belongingness, Listening, and Empathy that are the foundation for the Support pillar. These behaviors communicate "I've got your back." They transform support from a concept into a daily experience, one that builds trust, psychological trust, and team cohesion in the moments that matter most.

Support in Leadership:
Creating Psychological Trust

Exceptional leaders understand that support isn't about lowering expectations; it's about creating the conditions where people can meet high standards with confidence. Here's how they do it through CABLES Behaviors from Chapter 4:

Consistency (walking the talk) builds the foundation of trust. Angela Merkel, former Chancellor of Germany, earned broad respect through her steady leadership and calm decision making, even in high-pressure moments like the European financial crisis and the refugee influx. Her consistent tone, follow-through, and transparency gave people a sense of predictability in unpredictable times. Consistency isn't rigidity; it's dependability that allows teams to take risks, knowing their leader won't shift direction based on mood or pressure.

In virtual environments, consistency becomes even more crucial, because team members can't observe daily behavior patterns. Your reliability in virtual meetings, response time to digital messages, and follow-through on commitments become the primary signals people use to evaluate whether you have their back.

Belongingness creates inclusive environments. I've often suggested in my workshops with leaders the enormous responsibility they have to ensure that members of their team feel connected to the team and not feel as though they are looking in from the outside.

Creating belonging virtually requires fighting against proximity bias, where in-person team members naturally receive more attention and opportunities. Effective hybrid leaders develop systems to ensure equal inclusion regardless of physical location.

Listening transforms cultures. When Satya Nadella stepped into leadership at Microsoft, he led a cultural transformation by shifting the company from a "know-it-all" to a "learn-it-all" mindset. He modeled curiosity, asked thoughtful questions, and practiced authentic listening, signaling that insight can come from any level of the organization. Under his leadership, Microsoft's culture became more open, collaborative, and resilient.

Virtual listening requires extra effort to read nonverbal cues through screens, create space for voices that might get lost in group video calls, and establish multiple channels for team members to share ideas and concerns.

Empathy builds strength under pressure. When seven people died from cyanide-laced Tylenol capsules in 1982, Johnson & Johnson CEO James Burke led not just with business strategy, but with genuine concern for public trust. He immediately recalled 31 million bottles worth over $100 million, prioritizing human life over profit. His empathic leadership—putting people first, despite enormous financial consequences—demonstrated that empathy isn't weakness; it's strength that creates space where people can meet challenges as whole humans.

SUPPORTING DISTANT TEAMS: NEW LEADERSHIP CHALLENGES

Leading hybrid and remote teams requires adapting traditional support behaviors to virtual environments. The psychological trust that builds naturally through physical presence must be intentionally created across digital channels.

Virtual Consistency means maintaining reliable communication rhythms, consistent response times, and predictable meeting patterns. When team members can't see their leader daily, they rely heavily on consistent digital touchpoints to feel supported and connected.

Digital Belongingness requires deliberate inclusion strategies. Leaders must ensure remote workers get equal speaking time in meetings, equal access to informal conversations, and equal visibility in team communications. The casual hallway conversations that build belonging in traditional offices must be re-created through virtual coffee chats, online team building, and dedicated relationship time in meetings.

Remote Listening becomes more challenging but more important. Leaders must work harder to read virtual body language, create space for quieter voices in video calls, and establish multiple channels for team members to share ideas and concerns. Some people who speak up easily in person become quieter in virtual meetings, requiring leaders to actively invite participation.

Virtual Empathy means considering the unique challenges of remote work: home-environment distractions, technology frustrations, isolation, and the blurred boundaries between work and personal life. Leaders who practice empathy in virtual settings regularly check in about personal context and adjust expectations based on individual circumstances.

SUPPORT IN COACHING: BUILDING TRUST IN CHAOS

Coaching today isn't what it was even five years ago. As *The Price: What It Takes to Win in College Football's Era of Chaos* outlines so clearly, coaches are now navigating a volatile landscape shaped by NIL deals, transfer-portal dynamics, shifting loyalties, and growing outside influence.

As a former athlete and someone who works closely with teams, I don't pretend that any model is a complete answer to these systemic challenges. But I do believe the ideas presented here offer something essential that coaches still control: how they build connection, model values, and create a culture athletes want to be part of.

Support is often overlooked in coaching, yet it's one of the most critical behaviors for building trust. When athletes know their coach genuinely has their back, not just in performance but as individuals, they're more likely to stay engaged, take meaningful risks, and push through challenges.

CONSISTENCY: THE FOUNDATION COACHES CONTROL

John Wooden was an extraordinary leader. Although he never coached during the era of NIL deals or the transfer portal, his commitment to consistency would be more valuable than ever in today's unpredictable landscape. In a time when both coaches and players face constant uncertainty, Wooden's steady presence would have offered something rare: stability.

Research shows that consistent coaching strengthens motivation, trust, and identity. In a world that changes fast, consistency says, "This is a place you can count on."

BELONGINGNESS: MAKING EVERY PLAYER MATTER

Andy Reid showed what belonging looks like in one simple moment. In an interview, Donovan McNabb recalled being chewed out by Reid after a poor offensive series. As he turned to walk away, Reid shouted after him, "I love you." McNabb said that was the moment he knew his coach truly had his back. That combination of challenge and care built trust and connection far deeper than X's and O's.

That is the essence of belonging. It is not about overlooking mistakes or avoiding hard conversations. It is about making sure that, no matter what, players know they are valued for more than their performance.

This lesson is especially relevant in today's college-football environment. With NIL money and the transfer portal, athletes have more freedom and leverage than ever. By no means am I suggesting that belonging will outweigh the pull of significant NIL opportunities. But I will guarantee this: If a program fails to create belonging, it makes leaving that much easier. Money will always trump a lack of loyalty.

Coaches who fail to recognize this shift will find themselves at a disadvantage, while those who intentionally create belonging will hold onto something money cannot buy: commitment.

LISTENING: CREATING SPACE FOR ATHLETE VOICES

Anson Dorrance didn't just build a powerhouse program at UNC Women's Soccer. He built a culture of shared ownership. His "competitive cauldron" model didn't just track performance; it invited athletes into transparent conversations about growth, accountability, and leadership.

In today's environment, listening is no longer optional. Athletes have more to say and more platforms to say it on than ever before. When coaches create space for honest dialogue and truly listen, not just to respond but to understand, they earn something far more powerful than compliance: commitment.

EMPATHY: COACHING THE WHOLE PERSON

Tony Dungy was a different kind of NFL coach. He led with calm under pressure, spoke with purpose instead of volume, and built teams that won not just with talent but with trust. His leadership was rooted in dignity and emotional intelligence. He didn't just coach football players; he coached people.

For coaches today, empathy is essential. Athletes are managing more than just training loads; they're carrying mental-health pressures, identity exploration, family dynamics, and often public scrutiny. Empathy doesn't mean lowering the bar; it means being the kind of coach who understands what someone is carrying as they reach for it.

SUPPORT IN PARENTING: THE FOUNDATION FOR LIFE

It's been said that by the time a child turns eighteen, parents will have already spent about ninety to ninety-five percent of the total in-person time they'll ever have with that child. Whether or not that number is exact, the reality behind it is clear: The window to shape, support, and strengthen our children is shorter than it feels.

Families are not just important teams; they're the most lasting ones we'll ever be part of. Parents are the primary coaches and team leaders, setting the tone, creating the environment, and modeling the behaviors that shape how children relate to themselves and others.

CONSISTENCY: WALKING THE TALK WITH YOUR KIDS

Children thrive when they know what to expect. But consistency isn't just about bedtime schedules or house rules; it's about alignment. One of the things Cyndi and I tried hard to be consistent about as parents was how we responded when our kids—Grace, Josh, and Noah—came to us with something difficult. We told them often, "You can come to us about anything, especially the hard stuff."

But we knew that if the first time they came to us in high school about issues like drinking or peer pressure, and we immediately jumped into reprimanding or lecturing them, that door would close fast. Consistency for us meant showing them, over time, that we'd listen first, even when it was uncomfortable.

Now that they're adults, all three of them have said that made a big difference. They felt like they could come to us without fear of being shut down, and that helped us have real conversations when it mattered most.

Walking the talk is one of the most powerful and challenging ways we model support. If I expect my child to own their mistakes, I must be willing to own mine. If I want them to show patience or kindness, they must see those qualities in me first.

BEING A DIFFERENT KIND OF HELICOPTER PARENT

Support in parenting is not about solving every problem for your child; it's about sending the consistent message, through words and actions, that they are never alone in solving it. I often say I'm a helicopter parent, but not the kind most people think of. I don't hover. I don't shield my kids from every challenge or discomfort.

Instead, I see myself as part of an elite tactical-support unit ready to step in when there's a true emergency, but otherwise encouraging them to find their own way out of the woods. That's the real balance of support: being close enough for rescue, but far enough to let them build strength, solve problems, and grow. That's how kids learn we've got their back without holding them back.

LISTENING: THE CHALLENGE OF BEING PRESENT

One of the most powerful ways to support a child is simply to listen fully, without distraction, and without rushing to fix. When parents truly listen, they do more than gather information; they create connection.

But listening, especially as a parent, requires intentional effort. It means being present even when you're tired, curious even when you think you already know the answer, and patient even when you want to speed through the moment.

I'll be the first to admit this is easier said than done. There have been many times I've struggled to just listen without reacting. Usually, I know I've missed the mark when I see my kids shut down mid-conversation. It's a gut punch but also a reminder. We're not perfect, and we don't need to be. We just need to be consistent in trying. Listening is a practice, not a finish line.

When children know they can talk and be heard, they're more likely to keep talking as they grow. And that may be one of the most important forms of support a parent can offer. It is certainly one Cyndi and I are reaping the benefits from now, even with our parenting missteps.

SUPPORT IN RELATIONSHIPS: THE TEAM OF TWO

By definition, a couple is a team. And like any great team, success doesn't come from grand gestures. Success is built on a foundation of consistent support. When partners feel that they are seen, heard, and safe with one another, they operate with more trust, resilience, and emotional generosity.

The two-cars principle applies directly here. Support in a relationship doesn't mean solving each other's problems. It means creating a space where both people feel empowered to show up fully, especially when things are hard.

THE COFFEE-MOMENT PRINCIPLE

Small moments matter more than we realize. The previous coffee moment with Cyndi wasn't scheduled or planned. It was a choice to prioritize connection over productivity, presence over pressure. It's easy to get caught up in what feels urgent. But in the end, it's the small things, done consistently, that often matter most.

Here's what consistency looks like in everyday relationships: following through on plans, reacting predictably to conflict, making space for regular check-ins, and avoiding emotional whiplash where you're loving one moment and distant the next.

CREATING CONNECTION ACROSS DISTANCE

The spontaneous coffee moment Cyndi and I shared represents something that becomes much harder in virtual work environments: unplanned moments of connection. When teams are distributed, these relationship-building opportunities don't happen by accident. They must be intentionally created.

Virtual teams that build strong support systems understand they must design what used to occur naturally. This might mean scheduling "virtual coffee breaks," where work talk is off limits, creating online spaces for casual conversation, or establishing regular check-in calls that focus on personal connection rather than task updates.

The challenge is making these planned interactions feel genuine rather than forced. The most effective virtual leaders learn to read digital energy, notice when someone seems disconnected, and create informal opportunities for support and connection. They might send a private message asking "How are you really doing?" or suggest a brief one-on-one call that has nothing to do with work deliverables.

Remote team members also bear responsibility for creating connection. This means participating in virtual social opportunities, reaching out when they need support, and being intentional about building relationships with colleagues they may rarely see in person.

The key insight is that support in virtual environments requires more planning but can be just as meaningful as in-person connection. Teams that master this balance create strong bonds across physical distances, while those that leave connection to chance often struggle with isolation and disengagement.

The only time we can learn something new is when we listen. In hybrid teams, it's especially important to ensure that remote workers don't become "second-class citizens" who miss out on the spontaneous support moments that happen naturally among office-based team members. This requires conscious effort to include virtual participants in informal conversations and create equal opportunities for connection, regardless of physical location.

LEARNING TO LISTEN BETTER

One thing I've learned from Cyndi is that it's not always about solving the problem; it's about listening. Sometimes the most supportive thing we can do is simply be present. That's why asking a simple question, "Do you want to be helped or heard?" can make all the difference. It helps clarify your role in the conversation and ensures you show up in the way the other person actually needs.

Remember, the only time we can learn something new is when we listen, and every time we speak, we're only repeating what we already believe or think we know.

CREATING SHARED BELONGING

In strong relationships, partners don't just coexist; they co-create. This morning, while Cyndi and I sat on the porch, we weren't just drinking coffee. We were participating in one of our small rituals that reinforces our connection. Whether it's Sunday pancakes, evening walks, or shared grocery-shopping trips that become conversation time, small recurring experiences become emotional anchors.

When partners make decisions jointly, build rituals together, and speak in terms of "us" and "ours" rather than "I" and "you," they signal unity. This sense of belonging doesn't mean losing individuality. It means choosing to be part of something bigger.

EMPATHY WITHOUT AGREEMENT

Empathy in a relationship isn't about agreeing with everything your partner says. It involves making sure they don't feel alone in how they feel. It's the ability to step into their emotional world, even if you'd respond differently in the same situation.

When couples skip empathy and go straight to logic, defense, or solutions, they often miss the moment entirely. A response like, "That's not what happened," or "You're overreacting," may be factually true, but it's also invalidating. It makes your partner feel judged instead of supported.

Empathy doesn't require perfection. It just requires presence, patience, and the willingness to stay with someone in their experience, even when it's uncomfortable. Because when people feel emotionally safe, they're more likely to open up, resolve conflict constructively, and deepen intimacy.

The CABLES That Build Daily Support

While all six behaviors in the CABLES Model contribute to stronger relationships, these four create the foundation of support:

Consistency creates predictability people can count on. It's the leader who follows through, the coach who maintains standards fairly, the parent who responds reliably, and the partner who shows up emotionally.

Belongingness fosters the sense that "You matter here." It's making sure every voice is heard, every contribution is valued, and every person feels involved in the team's success.

Listening demonstrates respect and creates connection. It's putting the phone down, asking follow-up questions, reflecting instead of rushing to respond, and creating space for others to be heard.

Empathy validates experiences without requiring agreement. It's pausing to understand before seeking to be understood, staying present with someone's emotion, and responding with "I see you" before "Here's what you should do."

These behaviors, practiced consistently across all relationships, create the psychological trust that turns ordinary groups into extraordinary teasms.

The Foundation That Makes Everything Possible

Support is more than the first pillar of great teams. Support is the cornerstone that makes productive challenge possible. When people feel genuinely supported, they don't just engage more fully. They become more resilient, more open to feedback, and more willing to stretch beyond their comfort zone.

Whether you're leading a team, coaching athletes, raising children, or building a partnership, support is demonstrated through consistent daily actions that tell people: "I've got your back." It's not about perfection; it's about showing up reliably with the CABLES Behaviors that build trust, create connection, and foster psychological trust.

The most powerful teams, families, and relationships aren't built on talent alone; they're built on the deep trust that comes from mutual support. When that foundation is strong, everything else becomes possible.

But support alone isn't enough. People need more than trust; they need fuel. They need to feel not just supported, but seen and valued for their contributions. That's where the second pillar comes in: the power of celebration.

Key Takeaways

- Support builds psychological trust that enables engagement, risk taking, and collaboration.
- The "two-cars principle" shows that support means adjusting pace to stay connected, not always moving at the same speed.
- In virtual environments, support behaviors must be more intentional because casual connection opportunities don't happen accidentally.
- Support is demonstrated through daily CABLES Behaviors: Consistency, Belongingness, Listening, and Empathy.
- Small moments of support (like sharing coffee) often matter more than grand gestures.
- Virtual teams require deliberate design of connection opportunities that used to happen naturally in physical environments.
- True support balances rescue with growth, being close enough to help but far enough to let others develop strength.
- Support creates the foundation that makes productive challenge possible later.

Reflection Questions

- How consistently do I show up for others in small, daily moments?
- When someone needs support, do I ask, "Do you want to be helped or heard?"
- Where in my life am I trying to "solve" when I should be listening?
- How well do I practice the "two-cars principle" of adjusting my pace to stay connected with others?
- In virtual or hybrid settings, how am I being more intentional about creating connection opportunities?
- What small rituals of support could I build into my relationships?

Practice Prompt

Before moving on, identify one relationship where you could strengthen Support this week. Choose one CABLES Behavior (Consistency, Belongingness, Listening, or Empathy) to focus on, and practice it consistently for seven days. Notice how small, intentional acts of support begin to transform the trust and connection in that relationship.

Pay attention to moments like the coffee invitation. These aren't interruptions to important work; they are the important work of building relationships that make everything else possible.

What's Next

What happens when people feel truly seen and valued? They don't just show up differently. They become different. Support creates the foundation, but there's a second pillar that transforms that foundation into unstoppable momentum.

It's the fuel that keeps motivation alive and deepens people's commitment to the team's mission. Most teams completely miss its power, thinking recognition is just about making people feel good. They're wrong. It's about reinforcing the behaviors that lead to sustained excellence.

That's where we're headed next in Chapter 8: the power of Celebrate.

BLUEPRINT COMPONENT:
HOW TO BUILD THE CELEBRATE TOWER

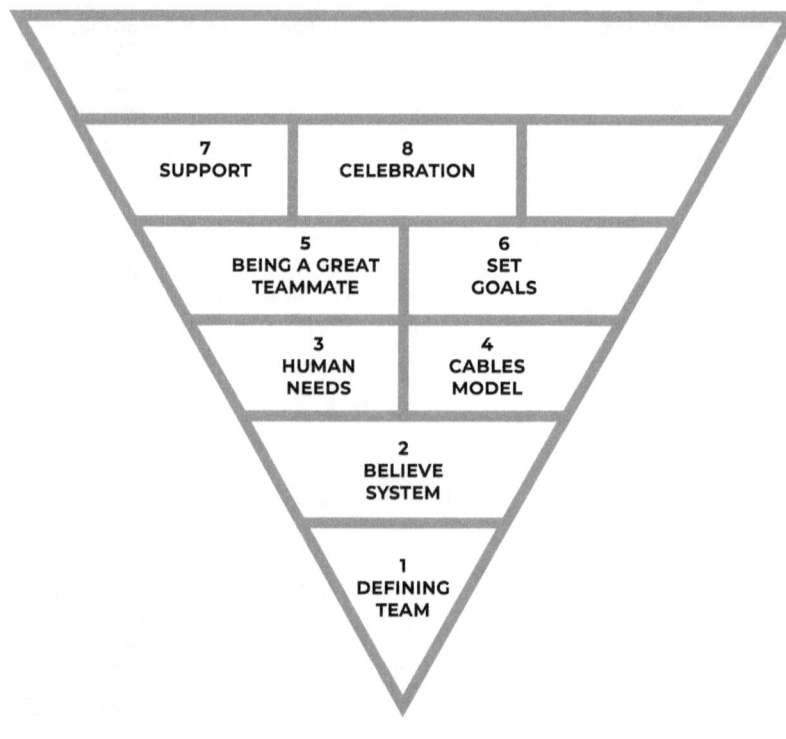

CHAPTER 8
WHY CELEBRATION MATTERS

"The deepest principle in human nature
is the craving to be appreciated."

– WILLIAM JAMES

Picture this: Your team just delivered an incredible quarter. Everyone contributed. The late nights, the creative problem solving, the way people stepped up when others were struggling. It was the kind of performance that happens when people truly work together.

And then... nothing. No acknowledgment. No recognition. Just straight into planning for next quarter.

Sound familiar?

That's why Celebrate is an individual pillar of great teams. And it's not about handing out participation trophies or empty praise. It's about reinforcing the behaviors and contributions that actually drive results.

Why Celebration Needs Its Own Pillar

Working and observing hundreds of teams across different industries and contexts, I have seen a clear pattern. Teams that master celebration consistently outperform those that do not, regardless of talent level. While support creates the foundation of trust, celebration fuels motivation and reinforces the specific behaviors that drive results. Yet, celebration often gets relegated to annual events or generic "good job" comments that fall flat.

The teams that overlook this pillar may achieve short-term results, but they struggle with retention, engagement, and sustained excellence. Great teams go beyond celebrating wins; they highlight the work, growth, and effort it takes to get there.

But here's what most teams average or struggling teams miss: recognition without substance feels hollow. When someone says "You're a rockstar" or

"Great job" without any specifics, the recipient often walks away thinking you don't really know what they did. That's not celebration; that's noise.

Just like support, celebration is not just one person's responsibility. Every team member—whether you are a manager, coach, parent, or partner—has the power to influence the environment by how you recognize and appreciate those around you.

The Science Behind Why Recognition Works

Celebration is a behavior that fuels engagement, deepens commitment, and drives sustained performance. There is a great deal of research that supports the variety of benefits that consistent timely and meaningful recognition plays in driving positive morale. One example is Gallup's Q12 survey. The Q12 ranks recognition among the strongest predictors of satisfaction, productivity, and retention. Another is *The Progress Principle* by Teresa Amabile and Steven Kramer. Their research shows that consistently acknowledging small wins is one of the most effective ways to sustain motivation.

Celebration is a behavior that fuels engagement, deepens commitment, and drives sustained performance.

Here's where the science matters. When someone receives authentic recognition, their brain releases dopamine, a neurochemical linked to learning, motivation, and memory. Dopamine encourages us to repeat behaviors that feel rewarding. This is why specific, genuine praise strengthens not just mood but momentum.

But the opposite is also true and often overlooked. When someone expects to be recognized for meaningful effort and is overlooked, the brain still reacts but not with motivation. It responds with social pain. Neurologically, the absence of expected recognition activates the same regions of the brain associated with physical pain and rejection. I have yet to work with a team where a comment is made that people feel like they are working really hard but are only told what they are not doing well. In this example, you can envision dopamine being syphoned out of people every time they experience this feeling of only being acknowledged for what they are not doing well.

The lesson? It's not just about adding motivation; it's about preventing withdrawal. When we fail to recognize real effort, people don't just feel unappreciated. They start to question whether their contributions matter at all.

The RPM Model:
Recognizing Positive Moments

In my training workshops, I teach a concept I call RPM: Recognizing Positive Moments. These are the RPMs that run the engagement engine in companies, teams, families, and relationships. Just like in a car, when RPMs are too low, the engine stalls. In human terms, that's disengagement. People go through the motions but without energy or enthusiasm.

When RPMs are too high, that's often when companies mandate engagement programs that seem insincere, and the engine burns out. Forced recognition programs, mandatory appreciation initiatives, or over-the-top celebration that doesn't feel authentic can actually backfire. This is often where the "eighth-place trophy" and "everyone gets a sticker" cynicism has originated.

The goal is to find the right RPM level: consistent, meaningful recognition that keeps the engagement engine running smoothly. Not so little that people disengage, not so much that it feels forced, but just the right amount to maintain motivation and momentum.

In hybrid and remote environments, the RPM model becomes even more critical because positive moments are less visible. The team member who stays late to help a colleague might go unnoticed when everyone works from different locations. The problem solved between virtual meetings doesn't get seen by others. Leaders must be more intentional about creating recognition systems that capture the invisible contributions happening in digital spaces.

Remote teams that maintain high engagement understand this amplified recognition challenge. They create systematic touchpoints for appreciation: digital appreciation platforms, video recognition messages, virtual celebration rituals, and online peer-nomination systems. They recognize that if appreciation isn't deliberately planned and executed in virtual environments, it often doesn't happen at all.

The RPM principle applies equally in distributed teams, but the delivery mechanisms require more purposeful design to ensure the engagement engine keeps running smoothly across physical distances.

Using CABLES to Create Meaningful Celebration

CONSISTENCY: CREATING EQUAL OPPORTUNITY FOR RECOGNITION

When it comes to celebrating people, consistency is one of the most important behaviors you can model, because consistency builds trust. People naturally pay close attention to who gets celebrated and why. When recognition feels inconsistent or unequal, it quickly undermines morale. But when your appreciation is consistent and everyone knows their contributions have an equal chance of being noticed, it sends a clear message: "Your effort matters here."

In virtual and hybrid environments, consistency is crucial because teammates can't observe your daily recognition patterns. When remote workers consistently miss out on casual appreciation or when in-person employees receive more frequent acknowledgment, these inconsistencies compound faster than in traditional office settings. Effective virtual leaders develop systems to ensure both remote and office-based team members receive equal recognition opportunities.

One simple system I share with leaders who want to build the habit of consistent appreciation is to schedule it. When I am working on developing a new behavior, I set calendar reminders daily at 10:30 a.m. and 3:00 p.m., with a trigger word that reminds me what I am working on developing. If I were working on celebrating people more, I might put the word *Appreciation* in my calendar alert. The first reminder prompts me to look for someone to recognize, and the second ensures I do not miss another opportunity before the end of the day. It is a simple system, but it creates the consistency that turns good intentions into lasting habits.

For distributed teams, this calendar system becomes even more valuable, because it creates deliberate touchpoints to recognize contributions that might otherwise go unnoticed in virtual environments. Some leaders use these reminders to rotate recognition across different team members, ensuring everyone receives attention regardless of their physical location or communication style.

Consistency builds momentum and trust. When recognition is predictable, individuals do not have to wonder if their efforts will be noticed. This trust creates powerful momentum, motivating people to keep giving their best.

APPRECIATION: SEEING PEOPLE FOR WHO THEY ARE

Appreciation is foundational. Without it, the rest feels hollow. Appreciation is not just about clapping for results. It requires *seeing* people, which involves recognizing not only what they *do*, but who they *are* while doing it.

I do not believe appreciation gets overlooked out of intentional neglect. I believe it happens because we are moving fast, solving problems, and assuming people "just know" we value them. Yet, most of the time, they do not. Not unless we tell them.

At work, appreciation often gets buried under urgency. The team member who volunteers for the tough shift, smooths over a customer issue before it escalates, or quietly mentors a new colleague gets overlooked. As a leader, those are the moments you have to *catch* and name. Not in a vague "good job" way, but with specificity: "The way you handled that today showed real ownership. That is exactly what we mean when we talk about accountability on this team."

The same holds true in athletic settings. Coaches often praise performance, stats, wins, clutch plays. But what about the athlete who shows up early, who brings energy to the locker room, who encourages teammates after a mistake? These contributions are cultural glue. When you recognize those less visible moments, you tell your athletes: "I/we do not just care about what you do; I/we care about how you show up for each other."

At home, appreciation often fades into routine. The child who always makes their bed, the one who helps a younger sibling, the teen who checks in after school without being reminded: these behaviors often go unacknowledged until they are missing. When you say, "I noticed how you helped your brother today without being asked. That is being a great teammate," you are not just reinforcing a behavior. You are shaping identity.

In relationships, appreciation often shows up in small, easily missed gestures. When you say something like, "Thank you for always making time to really listen. I know that takes effort, and I appreciate it," you breathe life back into the relationship.

BELONGINGNESS: MAKING SURE THEY KNOW THEY MATTER

Belongingness is about more than inclusion. It is about connection. It is about celebrating people in ways that tell them, "You matter here not just for what you do, but for who you are." At the core of belongingness is our ability to be genuinely happy for others, even when we are personally struggling. True belonging means saying, "I want you to succeed, and I will celebrate you, even if it is not my moment." That kind of mindset builds relationships rooted in trust, loyalty, and emotional trust.

There is a powerful African proverb that says, "The child who is not embraced by the village will burn it down to feel its warmth." It is a stark reminder that when people feel excluded or unseen, they may disengage, or worse, act out—not from malice, but from a deep human need to matter. Belonging is not a soft sentiment; it is a foundational need. When people feel they are truly part of something, they do not just show up. They invest, contribute, and grow.

Belongingness means people feel included in the celebration not because they are the loudest, the most successful, or the most likeable, but because they are part of the team, the family, or the relationship. Recognition that builds belongingness is personal. It acknowledges the unique contributions, perspectives, and strengths of each person.

In high school, I was named MVP of a big football game we won against a crosstown rival, Portland High School. The award was called The Duffy, and it was an award voted on and given annually to the top player. While I was proud to win it and believed I had earned it, my coach was quoted in the paper the next day saying someone else on our team should have won the award. That one comment undercut the moment and quietly told me I did not truly belong. Coaches have immense influence in how they celebrate players. Celebrating effort, character, and quiet leadership—not just points scored—helps every athlete know they are part of the team. That kind of inclusion builds trust and chemistry that lasts far beyond the game.

Belongingness can be tested most when others on the team are succeeding and you are in a slump. Can you genuinely say, "I see you succeeding, and I am happy for you," even when your own journey feels stuck? That is the true measure of maturity, connection, and leadership. Strong teams are built when individuals lift each other up—not just when they win together, but when they can celebrate one another, even from the sidelines.

Whether you are a coach, leader, parent, or partner, modeling this kind of response fosters an environment where everyone feels valued and where everyone wants to see others succeed. Recognition becomes powerful when it moves beyond results and speaks to belonging. It is not just about what someone did. It is more about who they are and how they show up for others. When we celebrate people not only for their performance but for their presence, effort, and character, we build emotional trust and deepen trust.

SPECIFICITY: MAKING RECOGNITION CRYSTAL CLEAR

This is where most recognition fails. When someone says, "You're a rockstar," or "Great job," the recipient often thinks you don't really know what they did. Generic praise feels hollow because it doesn't demonstrate that you actually noticed their specific contribution.

Instead of "Great presentation," try "Your presentation was effective because you used specific examples that helped everyone understand the complex data. That kind of clarity helps our entire team make better decisions."

Instead of "You did great on that project," try "Your analysis identified three cost-saving opportunities that saved us $50,000, and your presentation helped the entire executive team understand the implications. That's exactly the strategic thinking we need."

Instead of "You're such a good kid," try "When you helped your sister with her homework, even though you were tired, that showed real kindness and responsibility. That's the kind of character that makes me proud."

When you name exactly what someone did and why it mattered, several things happen: They know you were actually paying attention, they understand which behaviors to repeat, others who hear the recognition learn what excellence looks like, and the behavior gets reinforced and becomes more likely to continue.

Celebration Across All Your Roles

The power of celebration shows up differently across roles, but the underlying principles remain the same.

In Leadership: Alan Mulally transformed Ford's culture through weekly meetings where he intentionally recognized incremental progress, not just large successes. Doug Conant at Campbell Soup personally wrote over 30,000 thank-you notes to employees during his tenure, making each employee feel personally valued.

In Coaching: Steve Kerr publicly celebrates role players and incremental growth, intentionally spotlighting contributions often unnoticed. Pat Summitt celebrated effort and resilience during tough times to build athletes' confidence. When coaches say, "I noticed how you picked up your teammate after that mistake. That is what leadership looks like," they reinforce behaviors that build championship culture.

In Parenting: When parents celebrate children's effort, patience, kindness, and problem solving rather than just big outcomes, they foster a growth mindset. Process-based praise like "I love how patiently you worked through that difficult problem" develops lasting self-confidence and willingness to take on challenges.

In Relationships: When couples regularly celebrate each other, not just for big events but small moments of kindness, effort, and emotional support, their relationship deepens. When you say, "I noticed how patient you were with me tonight, even though you were tired. I really appreciate your kindness," you create emotional trust and deepen trust.

Common Implementation Challenges

Even when you understand the importance of celebration, several roadblocks can get in the way:

The Urgency Trap: When things get busy, recognition gets pushed aside. The solution is to make celebration systematic, not spontaneous. Use calendar reminders to ensure it doesn't get forgotten.

The Virtual Visibility Gap: In hybrid and remote environments, good work becomes less visible, making it easier for contributions to go unnoticed. Combat this by creating systematic recognition reviews, asking team members to highlight each other's contributions, and establishing regular forums for peer appreciation.

The Perfectionism Problem: Some hesitate to celebrate until results are perfect. But recognizing effort and progress actually accelerates improvement. When we only acknowledge perfect outcomes, people become reluctant to take risks.

The Sincerity Concern: The key is to be specific and authentic rather than elaborate. Instead of generic praise, name exactly what you noticed and why it mattered.

The Time Excuse: Meaningful recognition often takes less than thirty seconds. A specific, genuine comment in the moment is more powerful than an elaborate gesture later.

The Comparison Trap: Make recognition about individual growth and effort rather than relative performance. Instead of "You are our best performer," try "I noticed how much your skills have improved."

Building Your Recognition System

Here's how to make celebration systematic:

Daily: Use the calendar-reminder system. Set alerts at 10:30 a.m. and 3:00 p.m. with "Appreciation" as your trigger word. This maintains the right RPM level for your engagement engine. For virtual teams, use these reminders to rotate recognition across remote and in-person team members.

Weekly: Start meetings or family dinners by highlighting one person's effort, growth, or character. In virtual meetings, create dedicated time for appreciation where team members can recognize each other's contributions.

Monthly: Recognize someone for who they are, not just for what they accomplished. Acknowledge character traits that strengthen your team or relationship. Use digital platforms to create appreciation posts others can see and build upon.

Quarterly: Create opportunities for peer recognition. Let team members, family members, or partners acknowledge each other's contributions. For distributed teams, consider virtual appreciation events or digital recognition boards where people can celebrate each other.

The goal isn't perfection; it's consistency. Small, regular acts of recognition compound over time into cultures where people feel deeply valued and motivated to contribute their best.

Digital Recognition Strategies

For teams operating in hybrid or remote environments, celebration requires additional tools and systems:

Virtual Recognition Platforms: Use collaboration tools like Slack, Microsoft Teams, or dedicated recognition platforms to create public appreciation channels where team members can acknowledge each other's contributions in real time.

Video Appreciation Messages: Personal video messages feel more authentic than text-based recognition. Record short videos highlighting specific contributions and share them with individuals or teams.

Digital Celebration Rituals: Create virtual team celebrations for milestones, achievements, and progress. This might include online team lunches, virtual trophy presentations, or digital appreciation ceremonies.

Online Peer-Nomination Systems: Establish systems where team members can nominate each other for recognition, ensuring that good work gets noticed, even when leaders aren't directly observing it.

Virtual Office Hours: Schedule regular virtual "drop-in" times specifically for appreciation and recognition, creating dedicated space for celebration that might otherwise get lost in task-focused meetings.

The key is to make digital appreciation feel as personal and meaningful as in-person recognition while taking advantage of technology's ability to create permanent, shareable moments of celebration.

The Fuel That Sustains Excellence

Celebration is more than the second pillar of great teams. It is the fuel that keeps motivation alive when the work gets hard and results feel distant. When individuals feel genuinely recognized for their efforts, progress, and character, they don't just work harder; they work with greater purpose and resilience.

Whether you are leading a team, coaching athletes, raising children, or building a partnership, celebration is demonstrated through consistent recognition that tells people: "I see you, I value you, and your contributions matter." It is not about lowering standards or giving participation trophies. It is about reinforcing the behaviors and effort that lead to genuine excellence.

Remember the RPM model: You want to maintain consistent recognition that keeps the engagement engine running smoothly. The calendar-reminder system helps you find this sweet spot by creating consistent touchpoints for recognition without overwhelming anyone with artificial appreciation.

When you master celebration through consistency, appreciation, belongingness, and specificity, you create environments where people don't just perform—they thrive. And that transformation begins with your very next interaction.

Key Takeaways

- Celebration drives engagement and long-term motivation when it is meaningful, specific, and consistent.
- The RPM model helps you find the right level of recognition: not too little (disengagement) or too much (burnout).
- In virtual environments, positive moments become less visible, requiring more systematic recognition approaches.
- Generic praise ("You're a rockstar") feels hollow; specific recognition shows you were paying attention.
- The calendar-reminder system turns good intentions into consistent habits, especially important for distributed teams.
- Digital recognition tools and virtual celebration rituals can maintain team connection across physical distances.
- Celebrating progress and effort, not just outcomes, builds resilience and a growth mindset.
- Consistency in recognition creates trust and ensures everyone feels valued equally, regardless of location.
- Belongingness through celebration helps people feel seen for who they are, not just for what they produce.

Reflection Questions

- Am I consistently recognizing effort and progress, or only celebrating final outcomes?
- Do I make recognition specific enough that people understand exactly what they did well?
- Are there quiet contributors whose efforts I might be overlooking?
- In hybrid or remote settings, am I ensuring that virtual team members receive equal recognition opportunities?
- Is my recognition creating the right RPM level, or am I letting the engagement engine stall or burn out?
- What digital tools could I use to make appreciation more visible and systematic in virtual environments?

Practice Prompt

This week, implement the calendar-reminder system. Set alerts at 10:30 a.m. and 3:00 p.m. with the word "Appreciation." Use each reminder to recognize one specific contribution, focusing on character, effort, or impact. Make your recognition specific enough that the person knows you were actually paying attention to what they did. If you lead a virtual or hybrid team, ensure you're alternating recognition between remote and in-person team members. Notice how genuine celebration begins to shift the energy and engagement of those around you.

What's Next

You've built the foundation of trust through support. You've created the momentum of engagement through celebration. Now your team is ready for something that will either elevate them to greatness or reveal what's still missing.

Challenge is where great teams separate themselves from everyone else. It's where potential becomes performance, where comfort zones get shattered, and where people discover they're capable of more than they ever imagined. But here's the critical truth most teams miss: Challenge without the foundation you've built isn't growth. It's pressure. And pressure breaks people.

When you've earned the right to challenge through support and celebration, something extraordinary happens. People don't resist it. They welcome it. They seek it out. Because they know it's coming from belief, not judgment.

That's where we're headed next: the final pillar that uncovers the missing piece and transforms average teams into great ones.

BLUEPRINT COMPONENT:
HOW TO BUILD THE CHALLENGE TOWER

CHAPTER 9
WHY CHALLENGE COMES LAST

"Iron sharpens iron, and one person sharpens another."

– PROVERBS 27:17

During college, after both my parents had passed away, I was living with my brother Vin and his wife Nancy. As I prepared to head back for my junior year, I casually mentioned that I'd stolen an alarm clock from a store at the mall.

I'll never forget the look in Vin's eyes: shock, disappointment, and love all at once. He asked me what I was thinking, and I felt an overwhelming wave of embarrassment. The next day, I quietly returned the clock to the store.

Vin didn't shame me. He didn't lecture me. He challenged me, because he believed I was better than that. And here's the crucial part: He had already supported me by opening his home to me and celebrated me by believing in my potential. In that moment, his challenge helped me take ownership of my actions.

That's the difference between accountability and ownership. Accountability is external: people do what they're supposed to do because they have to. Ownership is internal: people take responsibility because they genuinely care.

This is why Challenge comes last. Without the foundation of Support and Celebration, Challenge feels like pressure. But when you've earned the right to challenge through connection and care, it becomes an invitation to grow.

The Accountability Paradox

Leaders often speak about accountability as though it is the ultimate measure of team effectiveness, but as I once shared in a LinkedIn article, accountability sets only the low bar. It's the floor. True team greatness emerges from ownership, which surpasses mere accountability.

Understanding the roots of these words reveals why. Accountability comes from the Old French *aconter*, meaning "to reckon" or "to answer for." It's about being called to account, about external measurement and judgment. Ownership, by contrast, stems from "possession," something you hold as your own. One is imposed from outside; the other comes from within.

This distinction explains why average and struggling teams get trapped in what I call the "accountability paradox." When performance falters, whether in organizations, sports teams, families, or personal relationships, the instinctive response is to impose another layer of accountability. More rules. Stricter monitoring. Clearer consequences. But this approach typically pushes people further away from taking ownership. The more you try to force accountability, the more you create compliance at best and resistance at worst. People do the minimum required because they have to, not because they want to.

Creating great teams is not about enforcing rules, although that happens. It is about inspiring commitment and shared responsibility to follow the rules: ownership. That said, this level of commitment does not happen by chance. Ownership must be carefully cultivated by first establishing trust through Support and reinforcing motivation and morale through Celebrate. Only then can Challenge be introduced effectively as a powerful tool for growth.

Average and struggling teams focus on accountability. They create rules, enforce consequences, and monitor compliance. People do what they're supposed to do because they have to, because someone is keeping a reckoning of their performance. But great teams have discovered something deeper: they create ownership. When people take genuine responsibility not just for their role but for the collective success of the team, something extraordinary happens. Standards rise not because someone is watching, but because people care. They possess a stake in the outcome.

This transformation doesn't happen by accident. Ownership can only be earned through the precise sequence we've explored: Support creates the psychological trust that allows people to invest fully. Celebrate builds the emotional connection that makes people want to contribute. Only then does Challenge become an invitation to grow rather than external pressure to perform.

When you have ownership, accountability is automatically present. People hold themselves and each other to high standards because they're personally invested in the outcome. But if you try to build accountability first, without the foundation of support and celebration, you'll rarely experience true ownership. You end up with a team constantly being called to account, constantly reckoning with external standards, but never truly possessing responsibility for the results.

Think of it like the Queensferry Crossing in Scotland I mentioned at the beginning of the book. This engineering marvel has three massive towers, each capable of carrying tremendous weight. While each tower is impressive on its own, it's the connections between them that make the bridge able to support incredible loads and positively impact all those who rely on this bridge. Support and Celebrate are like the outer towers: essential and powerful individually. Challenge is the central tower. But without the connecting sections linking all three together, the structure remains incomplete. The potential exists, but the bridge cannot serve its purpose.

That's exactly what happens with teams. Support, Celebrate, and Challenge only achieve their full strength when properly connected in the right sequence. When they work together, something powerful emerges: the missing piece that transforms teams from good to great. That connection creates ownership, the shift from being held to account to taking possession of responsibility. That's the missing piece.

The Power and Purpose of Effective Challenge

Once people feel supported and genuinely appreciated, something important happens: they become more open to being challenged. And not just challenged in the sense of being held accountable, but in a way that calls them to grow. That is what real leadership is about. It is not pointing out what is wrong, but calling out what is possible. It is saying, "I see more in you or in us, and I am committed to you and us reaching it."

It is not pointing out what is wrong, but calling out what is possible.

Real challenge calls us higher, and ownership is the result. It is here that the proper application and sequence of Support and Celebrate reveal the missing piece: the creation of ownership.

Too often, leaders skip the groundwork. They go straight to Challenge without building trust through Support and Celebrate. The result? People don't hear belief in what is possible, they hear judgment for what is not. Instead of stepping up, they shut down. I have seen this pattern happen across industries, from locker rooms to boardrooms to kitchen tables: When challenge comes without connection, it is taken as criticism, and ownership remains missing.

This is where great teams start to separate themselves from those that are average or struggling—both in how they perform and how they think. Average teams rely on accountability, rules, deadlines, and consequences to keep people in line. Great teams move past that. They operate from ownership. That is the shift from doing something because you have to, to doing it because you want to. Because it matters to you. Because it matters to the team.

If you want a great team, do not just look for compliance. Build connection first. Celebrate what is working. Then challenge each other to grow, not out of pressure, but out of belief in the value of each other. That is where the real transformation happens.

Why Challenge Without Foundation Becomes Pressure

When I think about effective challenge, I remember another lesson from my coaching work. Several years ago, I had the privilege of interviewing John Jennings, who served as an assistant basketball coach for the Boston Celtics during Red Auerbach's tenure. Jennings shared an insightful story highlighting Auerbach's unique approach to coaching different personalities.

Danny Ainge thrived on direct, assertive feedback; it energized and drove him to improve. Conversely, Robert Parish responded best to a more subtle, supportive form of communication. Auerbach understood this crucial distinction, tailoring his challenge style accordingly to draw out the best in each player. This story underscores a foundational principle in effective coaching: Recognizing and adapting to individual personality styles significantly enhances motivation and performance.

This connects directly to why the sequence matters. Challenge without relationship becomes pressure. Challenge with relationship becomes growth.

Our brains are wired to respond differently when we feel safe versus threatened. Neurologically, humans are wired to seek connection and belonging; feeling isolated or disconnected activates threat responses in the brain, reducing our ability to accept feedback openly and engage constructively. Conversely, when we feel genuinely connected and valued as part of a group, our brains respond positively, creating the ideal conditions to accept challenge as an opportunity rather than a threat.

When someone feels psychologically safe and valued, challenge activates growth centers in the brain. When someone feels unsafe or unappreciated, the same challenge activates threat responses, leading to defensiveness and resistance.

> When challenge comes without connection, people shut down rather than step up.

When challenge comes without connection, people shut down rather than step up. But when challenge is built on a foundation of support and celebration, people welcome it, because they know it comes from belief, not judgment. Without belongingness, even well-intentioned challenge can feel harsh and isolating, making individuals defensive and resistant.

The Virtual Challenge: When Distance Amplifies Pressure

Challenge becomes particularly complex in hybrid and remote environments, because the subtle cues that help people interpret feedback as supportive rather than critical often get lost in virtual communication. When someone receives challenging feedback through a screen, they miss the nonverbal reassurance that usually accompanies constructive criticism: body language, tone nuances, and the immediate opportunity for clarification.

Virtual challenge conversations require more deliberate foundation-building because team members can't rely on casual interactions to reinforce the Support and Celebrate pillars. A manager who rarely connects with remote employees beyond task updates will find that challenge conversations feel harsh and disconnected, even when delivered with good intentions.

Effective virtual leaders understand they must overcommunicate support and celebration to create sufficient foundation for productive challenge. They schedule regular relationship-building conversations, use video calls for important feedback discussions, and ensure that challenging conversations include explicit reminders of the person's value and potential. What might be implied through physical presence must be explicitly stated in virtual environments.

The CATCH Model becomes even more valuable in remote settings, because it provides structure that prevents virtual challenge conversations from feeling abrupt or disconnected from ongoing relationship building.

The Hidden Barriers to Effective Challenge

Over the years working with all types of teams, I've identified several unconscious biases that significantly reduce the effectiveness of challenge. I stress the word "unconscious" because these biases operate below our level of awareness so much so that most of us would quickly deny we even have them. Recognizing they exist is essential, because only when we are aware of these hidden tendencies can we effectively address and mitigate them.

CONFIRMATION BIAS:
WE SEE WHAT WE EXPECT TO SEE

Confirmation bias is our unconscious tendency to notice, interpret, and remember things in a way that confirms what we already believe, while disregarding contradictory evidence. For example, if I believe a team member is disengaged, I might subconsciously highlight every missed detail or late arrival, completely overlooking instances where they show initiative or engagement.

When we are unaware of this bias, it leads to unfair treatment and unequal standards. One person's mistakes get amplified, while another person's similar errors are overlooked. This creates resentment, resistance, and defensiveness. The key to challenging effectively is to intentionally look for information that challenges our assumptions, providing balanced feedback and treating everyone with equal treatment.

FUNDAMENTAL ATTRIBUTION ERROR:
MISJUDGING THE REASONS BEHIND ACTIONS

Another unconscious bias that comes up regularly is the fundamental attribution error, which is our tendency to attribute our own shortcomings to external circumstances while assuming others' shortcomings result from internal character flaws. If I miss a deadline, it is because I was overloaded; if you miss a deadline, it is because you are disorganized or unfocused.

This bias creates a disconnect during challenge conversations, making feedback feel accusatory rather than supportive. People naturally become defensive because they feel personally attacked rather than constructively coached. To overcome this, we need to actively pause, reflect, and genuinely inquire about situational factors rather than assuming negative intentions or capabilities.

In virtual environments, this bias becomes particularly problematic, because we have less context about what team members are dealing with at home. The person who seems disengaged during a video call might be managing childcare interruptions, technology issues, or inadequate workspace conditions rather than lacking motivation.

DUNNING-KRUGER EFFECT:
OVERESTIMATING OR UNDERESTIMATING ABILITIES

The Dunning-Kruger effect describes the phenomenon where individuals with lower competence in a particular area tend to overestimate their abilities, while those who are highly competent often underestimate their own skills. Within a team, this means some individuals resist challenge because they genuinely do not see their gaps, whereas others might shy away from stretching themselves, mistakenly believing they are not yet ready for greater responsibility.

When delivering challenge, if we do not recognize this unconscious bias, our approach may unintentionally provoke defensiveness or fail to provide the necessary encouragement. Being aware of this tendency helps us tailor our feedback, using direct, clear conversations to help some individuals see their blind spots and supportive encouragement to help others recognize their readiness for increased responsibilities.

Building Your Challenge Foundation Through CABLES

To implement effective challenge, five essential CABLES Behaviors create the foundation for productive challenge conversations. Successful Challenge, more than any other pillar, depends heavily on the strength and depth of our relationship bridges. If we are to ask others to step outside their comfort zones, to push beyond what feels easy or familiar, our relational foundations with them must be exceptionally strong.

CONSISTENCY: WALKING THE TALK

Consistency, at its core, is about personal accountability and credible modeling. Its significance in the context of challenge cannot be overstated. Before we can credibly challenge someone else to grow, improve, or stretch beyond their current limits, we must first consistently demonstrate those behaviors ourselves. If we ask others to take risks, meet high standards, or accept feedback, but fail to consistently hold ourselves to the same expectations, our credibility quickly erodes. Consistency is what turns our words into meaningful action, lending legitimacy to our challenge and establishing the trust necessary for others to willingly embrace the discomfort of growth.

In virtual team settings, consistency becomes even more critical, because team members can't observe daily behavior patterns. Your punctuality to virtual meetings, response time to messages, and follow-through on digital commitments become the primary consistency signals people use to evaluate your credibility when delivering challenge.

BELONGINGNESS: BUILDING CONNECTION FOR EFFECTIVE CHALLENGE

Belongingness is the foundational sense of connection and psychological trust crucial for challenge to be truly effective. Neurologically, humans are wired to seek connection and belonging; feeling isolated or disconnected activates threat responses in the brain, reducing our ability to accept feedback openly and engage constructively. Conversely, when we feel genuinely connected and valued as part of a group, our brains respond positively, creating the ideal conditions to accept challenge as an opportunity rather than a threat. Without belongingness, even well-intentioned challenge can feel harsh and isolating, making individuals defensive and resistant.

Digital environments can make connection feel more effortful, requiring leaders to be more intentional about creating belongingness before attempting to challenge. Virtual team members who feel disconnected from their colleagues will interpret challenge differently than those who feel genuinely included and valued as part of the team.

LISTENING: AUTHENTIC UNDERSTANDING TO INFORM CHALLENGE

Authentic listening is essential for effective challenge because it demonstrates genuine respect and creates clarity about the nature of the challenge itself. It involves all four aspects of the Authentic-Listening Model: listening with your eyes, ears, mind, and respect. Listening with your eyes means observing nonverbal cues and understanding what might be left unsaid. Listening with your ears involves actively hearing not just the words, but the tone, emotion, and underlying messages. Listening with your mind requires seeking genuine understanding and setting aside personal biases or preconceived judgments. Lastly, listening with respect emphasizes valuing the speaker's perspective, even when it differs from your own. Without authentic listening, we risk challenging others based on incomplete or incorrect assumptions, potentially damaging trust and effectiveness.

In virtual challenge conversations, listening becomes more challenging but more important. Leaders must work harder to read digital body language, create space for full expression, and ensure they understand the complete context before delivering feedback.

EMPATHY: UNDERSTANDING OTHERS' CHALLENGES TO ENCOURAGE GROWTH

Empathy plays a critical role in effectively challenging others, because it acknowledges the reality that everyone experiences slumps and faces personal and professional hurdles. While it is essential to push one another toward higher standards and growth, doing so without empathy can quickly undermine trust and confidence. Empathy requires us to step outside our own perspectives, making a deliberate effort to understand and consider the challenges someone else might be facing.

When we lead with empathy, we demonstrate genuine care and support, creating an environment where people feel seen and understood. This approach reduces defensiveness and increases receptivity, ensuring that challenge becomes a productive opportunity for improvement rather than a stressful burden.

Remote work contexts require additional empathy for home-environment factors, technology limitations, and the unique challenges of maintaining work-life boundaries when teams are distributed across different locations and time zones.

SPECIFICS: CLARIFYING EXPECTATIONS FOR MEANINGFUL CHALLENGE

Specificity is crucial for effective challenge because it creates clarity around expectations and accountability. Without clear, explicit expectations, individuals can become uncertain about what is needed or expected from them, leading to confusion, frustration, and decreased effectiveness. Clearly defined specifics not only outline what each person should do but also emphasize the necessity of following through on commitments made. This ensures mutual accountability and trust, creating an environment where everyone understands their role, the goals they are aiming for, and how their contributions matter. By establishing and reinforcing clear expectations, specifics eliminate ambiguity, enabling challenges to become powerful tools for targeted, meaningful growth rather than sources of misunderstanding or conflict.

Virtual environments eliminate many of the informal check-ins and clarifying conversations that happen naturally in traditional office settings, making written and verbal specificity even more critical for distributed teams.

When these CABLES Behaviors are consistently modeled, challenge interacts positively with the core human needs in our NEEDS Model. Challenge is not simply about pushing someone toward higher performance; it is intricately connected to either satisfying or undermining the fundamental needs we all share. When these needs are intentionally supported through CABLES Behaviors, challenge remains productive, fostering an environment where motivation thrives, resistance fades, and genuine growth emerges.

The CATCH Model:
Productive Challenge in Action

Effective teams understand the importance of addressing concerns promptly and constructively before they escalate. The CATCH Model provides a clear, structured approach to challenge that builds relationships while promoting growth. This simple yet powerful model emphasizes early intervention, clear communication, and collaborative problem solving.

C: Call out the Behavior. Begin by clearly identifying the specific behavior you've observed. Use objective, neutral language to avoid defensiveness and focus on the behavior itself rather than personal attributes.

A: Address the Frequency. Is there a pattern or not? If so, calmly and factually acknowledge how often this behavior has occurred. This helps individuals understand it's not a single, isolated event but a recurring issue needing attention.

T: Talk About the Impact. Explain clearly and respectfully the impact this behavior is having on team effectiveness, productivity, morale, or relationships. Focusing on impact makes the issue relevant and tangible, emphasizing why it matters.

C: Check for Other Issues. Invite the individual to openly discuss what might be contributing to the behavior. Practice authentic listening, showing genuine empathy and interest in understanding their perspective, challenges, or circumstances.

H: Help Identify Solutions. Together, explore and agree upon possible solutions or next steps. Focus on actions that are achievable, clearly defined, and supported by mutual understanding. This collaborative approach builds ownership and accountability.

The benefits of the CATCH Model include early intervention that addresses concerns promptly, preventing escalation. Constructive communication maintains respect and openness, avoiding blame. The collaborative approach promotes a positive environment through mutual problem solving. Supportive interaction strengthens relationships and trust, enhancing team cohesion.

CATCH MODEL IN VIRTUAL ENVIRONMENTS

The CATCH Model becomes particularly valuable for virtual teams because it provides structure for difficult conversations that might otherwise feel disconnected or harsh through digital channels. When challenging conversations happen over video or phone, the model ensures all important elements are covered systematically.

Virtual CATCH conversations require additional preparation: ensuring good audio/video quality, choosing appropriate timing across time zones, and following up with written summary to confirm mutual understanding. The "Check for Other Issues" step becomes especially important in remote settings, because home-environment factors might be contributing to performance challenges.

CATCH MODEL IN PRACTICE

EXAMPLE 1: VIRTUAL MEETING ENGAGEMENT

Call out the Behavior: "I've noticed that during our team video calls, you often have your camera off and seem less engaged in discussions."

Address the Frequency: "This has happened on our last two weekly team meetings."

Talk About the Impact: "When team members aren't visibly engaged, it affects group energy and makes it harder for others to read reactions and build on ideas."

Check for Other Issues: "Is there a particular reason you haven't been on with your camera?" Could it be technical? Have they been sick and don't want to be seen?

Help Identify Solutions: "What needs to happen going forward so you can be on the calls with the camera?"

EXAMPLE 2: MISSED DEADLINES

Call out the Behavior: "I have observed that deadlines for project deliverables have been missed recently."

Address the Frequency: "This has occurred with two important tasks this month."

Talk About the Impact: "Missing deadlines impacts the team's workflow and our ability to meet client expectations."

Check for Other Issues: "Is everything okay with you?" "Are there any unusual challenges or obstacles you have faced with these assignments? I would like to understand the situation better."

Help Identify Solutions: "What can we do to make sure this does not become a pattern?"

The CATCH Model works because it addresses issues early, maintains respect and openness, promotes collaborative problem solving, and strengthens relationships rather than straining them. Implementing the CATCH Model regularly helps create a culture where feedback is seen as a supportive, growth-oriented practice rather than a negative or punitive measure.

Challenge That Builds Character:
Lessons From Great Coaches

While recognizing that every coach has their human imperfections, the following coaches exemplify how effectively embracing constructive challenge can transform teams, athletes, and organizational cultures. These coaches demonstrate leadership practices that harness the power of challenge positively and productively.

Nick Saban built a reputation on relentless standards and unwavering expectations. He set clear performance metrics and followed through with consistency. But what stood out to me most wasn't just how he challenged athletes to improve on the field; it was how he held them accountable off the field in ways that shaped their character.

I remember watching an interview with former Alabama running back Damien Harris. He shared a story that left a lasting impression on me. One Friday morning during his senior year, Harris showed up late to a walkthrough because he had overslept. Coach Saban said nothing at the time, but on Saturday, just before the game, he told Harris he wouldn't be starting. Not because he had been late, but because he never came forward to take responsibility for it.

That moment wasn't about punishment: it was about teaching. Saban was showing that accountability isn't just about following rules; it's about owning your choices and having the integrity to face them directly. Harris later said it was one of the most important lessons he learned—not just in football, but in life.

This is what real challenge looks like. It's not about being hard for the sake of being hard. It's about pushing people to be better: not just athletes, but better teammates, better leaders, and better humans.

When Challenge Strengthens Relationships

In my own relationship with Cyndi, we have experienced our share of disagreements and challenging moments. However, it is clear to me that our ability to effectively navigate these times hinges on our consistent efforts in modeling the pillars of Support and Celebrate. Knowing we genuinely have each other's backs (Support) and regularly acknowledging each other's contributions and accomplishments (Celebrate) has allowed us to approach challenges constructively.

Without these pillars firmly in place, challenging conversations could easily become destructive, highlighting faults rather than fostering mutual growth and deeper connection.

In workshops with leaders experiencing difficulties with employees, I often start by pointing out that no manager, on the day they hire someone, eagerly anticipates the moment they will need to place that employee on a performance plan. Similarly, no new employee excitedly begins their first day thinking about when they will lose engagement or enthusiasm for their job. This principle equally applies to personal relationships. When couples stand at the altar reciting vows, they rarely think to themselves, "I cannot wait until we stop getting along or consider divorce."

Though often met with laughter, this illustrates an important truth: We enter relationships with the very best intentions, unaware that incremental shifts in behavior, even by just one percent, can gradually lead us away from our initial commitment and connection until, suddenly, serious issues emerge.

That's why consistently practicing Support and Celebrate is essential in any relationship. Without them, challenges can slip into blame and erode connection. But when people feel valued and secure, challenges become chances to grow together. In strong relationships, Challenge isn't about pointing out flaws; it's about helping each other become better.

Some of the most damaging relationship patterns aren't always loud or obvious: They often build slowly through everyday habits. Avoiding conflict might seem like a path to peace, but it often silences honest communication, leaving issues unresolved and resentment to grow beneath the surface. When one partner constantly focuses on what's wrong, offering criticism without appreciation, it chips away at self-esteem and weakens the connection. Public confrontations only add to this tension, turning private pain into public embarrassment and breaking trust.

Strong relationships are built on behaviors that reinforce trust and connection. Approach challenges with respect and empathy in even the hardest conversations. Set clear expectations together so responsibilities and boundaries are understood, not assumed. Balance your feedback by affirming your partner's strengths while offering thoughtful critique: this fosters growth without diminishing confidence. Address sensitive topics privately to protect dignity and build mutual trust.

CATCH MODEL FOR RELATIONSHIPS

The CATCH Model provides couples with a compassionate and structured framework for proactively addressing relational challenges. Its effectiveness lies in addressing small issues early, preventing them from escalating into significant conflicts. This method accommodates diverse communication styles, offering a safe approach for both assertive and conflict-averse individuals.

Common Challenge Mistakes to Avoid

Even the most well-intentioned leaders can unintentionally undermine their team's motivation and growth through ineffective challenge behaviors. Being aware of these common pitfalls helps leaders recognize their own actions and understand how these behaviors might negatively impact others, despite positive intentions.

Micromanagement involves excessive oversight and detailed control, leading people to feel distrusted and undervalued. The unintended consequence is reduced autonomy, diminished motivation, and increased disengagement.

Constant criticism means regularly highlighting minor mistakes without balanced recognition, which erodes confidence. Over time, this constant critique creates fear of failure, reduces risk taking, and stifles creativity and innovation.

Inconsistent standards occur when challenges are applied differently among team members, fostering perceptions of unequal treatment. This inequity can lead to resentment, diminished morale, and ultimately create divisions within the team.

Ambiguous expectations cause confusion and frustration. Without clarity, people struggle to prioritize effectively, reducing productivity and increasing anxiety about meeting uncertain standards.

Public criticism involves addressing performance issues or delivering challenges in front of others, which can humiliate individuals, damaging their dignity and causing defensiveness or withdrawal rather than constructive responses.

Avoiding difficult conversations allows problematic behaviors to continue unchecked. Over time, this avoidance diminishes team effectiveness, increases resentment among higher performers, and undermines respect for leadership.

These examples clearly illustrate common missteps in challenging others, highlighting how seemingly minor misjudgments can significantly impact team dynamics, engagement, and overall organizational effectiveness.

The Master Blueprint of Great Teams:
Understanding the Construction Process

Just like the Queensferry Crossing required massive crews, resources, and years of intensive construction to build, creating a great team demands the most significant investment of time and energy at the beginning. The initial phase of building Support, Celebrate, and Challenge requires focused effort, consistent attention, and deliberate action from leaders, coaches, parents, and partners.

But here's the encouraging truth: Once these three pillars are solidly established and properly connected, they don't require the same massive construction effort to maintain. Just like the Queensferry Crossing now operates with a much smaller maintenance crew compared to the army of workers who built it, great teams can sustain their excellence with ongoing care rather than constant reconstruction.

This connects directly to the One Percent Principle we discussed at the beginning of this journey. Remember, every day your team is getting one percent better or one percent worse. The construction phase is about making significant positive investments that establish the foundation. The maintenance phase is about consistent daily choices that preserve and strengthen what you've built.

The beauty of this approach is that once people experience genuine ownership—once they've felt the power of working on a team where Support, Celebrate, and Challenge flow naturally—they become invested in maintaining that culture themselves. They don't want to go back to environments characterized by compliance, fear, or indifference.

Think about the bridge again. Once the connections were made between the three towers, something remarkable happened. The structure gained integrity that made it self-reinforcing. Weight distributed properly. The bridge could handle traffic flowing in both directions. It became functional, not just impressive.

The same thing happens when teams achieve true ownership. The structure becomes self-reinforcing. People support each other without being asked. They celebrate each other's growth naturally. They challenge each other constructively because they're invested in collective success. The missing piece—ownership—emerges not as something you impose, but as something that develops organically from the foundation you've built.

But just like any bridge requires ongoing maintenance to ensure trust and functionality, great teams need consistent care to maintain their strength. The daily one percent choices still matter. Leaders still need to model CABLES Behaviors. Recognition still needs to happen regularly. Difficult conversations still need to be handled with care. The difference is that these become natural extensions of an established culture rather than forced interventions in a struggling one.

THE TRANSFORMATION CATALYST

Challenge becomes the catalyst that transforms average or struggling into great, precisely because it's connected by Support and Celebrate. Whether you are leading a team, coaching athletes, raising children, or building a partnership, effective Challenge demonstrates one consistent message: "I believe in your potential, and I am committed to helping you reach it."

When your team discovers this missing piece—when they move from doing their job to owning the mission—you'll see the difference immediately. People start seeking feedback instead of avoiding it. They help each other without being asked. They push beyond expectations not because they have to, but because they can't imagine doing anything less.

Just like the Queensferry Crossing, once all three pillars are connected, it can carry weight in both directions. Teams can move forward through challenge and growth, and they can also look back with appreciation for how far they've come. They can handle the traffic of daily operations and the occasional heavy loads of crisis or opportunity.

Challenge creates the conditions where people choose to stretch themselves, because they trust your intentions and believe in the process. The sequence of Support, Celebrate, and Challenge is the proven pathway that moves teams from accountability to ownership, from compliance to commitment, and from good performance to extraordinary results.

That's the missing piece. That's what great teams really do. And once you've built it, you don't have to keep building it—you just have to keep maintaining it through the daily one percent choices that preserve the culture you've created.

Key Takeaways

- Challenge is most effective when built on a foundation of Support and Celebrate.

- The goal is not accountability; it is Ownership, where people take internal responsibility for growth and results.

- Like the Queensferry Crossing, Support and Celebrate must be built on both sides before Challenge in the center can be effective.

- The greatest effort goes into building great teams initially; once established, they require maintenance rather than reconstruction.

- Virtual environments require more deliberate challenge approaches, because subtle supportive cues can get lost in digital communication.

- Unconscious biases can undermine even well-intentioned challenge: awareness is the first defense.

- Five CABLES Behaviors are essential for effective challenge: Consistency, Belongingness, Listening, Empathy, and Specificity.

- The CATCH Model provides a practical framework for constructive, relationship-building challenge across all environments.

- Individual differences matter. Adapt your approach based on personality styles and circumstances.

- Challenge should strengthen relationships, not strain them. If it creates resistance, examine your approach.

- The transformation from accountability to Ownership is the missing piece that separates great teams from average ones.

- Once Ownership emerges, the culture becomes self-reinforcing through daily one percent positive choices.

Reflection Questions

- Am I modeling the behaviors I expect from others, or challenging from a position of inconsistency?
- Do people feel psychologically safe and valued before I challenge them to grow?
- Am I listening to understand the full context before offering challenge or feedback?
- How do I ensure my challenge is building people up rather than tearing them down?
- What unconscious biases might be affecting how I challenge different people?
- In virtual settings, am I creating sufficient foundation through Support and Celebrate before attempting to Challenge?
- Am I moving people toward Ownership, or just enforcing accountability?
- Have I built strong enough foundations of Support and Celebrate to make Challenge effective?

Practice Prompt

This week, identify one person who would benefit from constructive challenge. Before approaching them, ensure you have established support and offered recent celebration. Then use the CATCH Model to address the issue in a way that strengthens your relationship while promoting their growth. Notice how challenge feels different when it is built on trust and delivered with genuine care.

What's Next

You now possess the complete framework for building great teams. You understand the NEEDS that drive human engagement, the CABLES Behaviors that strengthen relationships, and the three pillars—Support, Celebrate, and Challenge—that create the missing piece: Ownership.

But frameworks don't build great teams. People do. And specifically, people who are committed to turning insight into consistent action.

In Chapter 10, we'll focus on the most critical step of all: implementation. Because understanding what great teams do is only valuable if you can consistently apply these principles in your daily leadership, coaching, parenting, and relationships. You'll discover how to overcome the predictable obstacles that derail most change efforts and create lasting transformation in any environment you're part of.

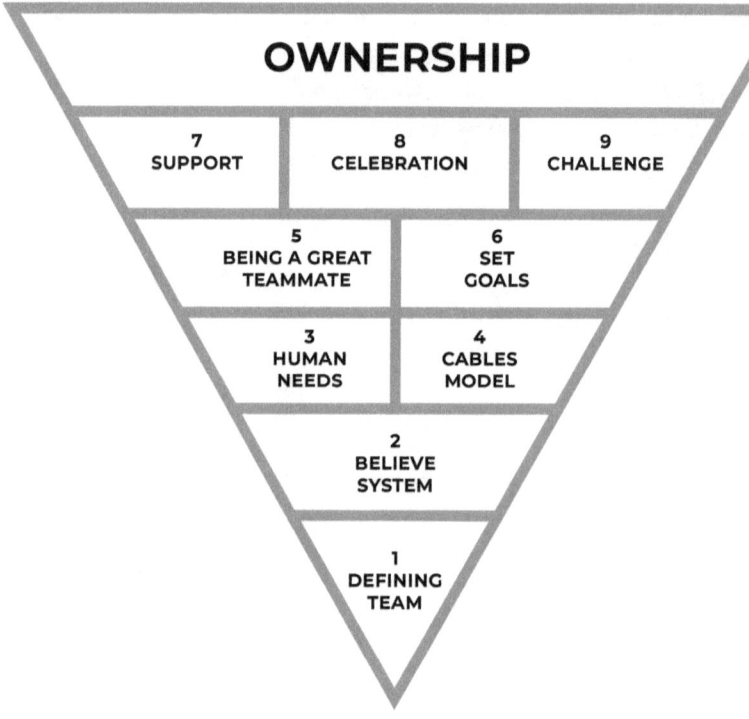

CHAPTER 10
TURNING INSIGHT INTO ACTION: OWNERSHIP UNCOVERED

"If you want to go fast, go alone.
If you want to go far, go together."

– AFRICAN PROVERB

You now have everything you need to build a great team. You have the master blueprint.

You've made it to the final chapter for a reason. You care about building something great and believe it is worth the investment. You care about how you lead, how you show up, and how your team performs. This book has given you the tools, the models, and the mindset. Now the most important work begins: consistent application.

This part of the master blueprint is about what needs to happen to complete the build and maintain it so it does not slip into disrepair.

The Implementation Challenge

If great teams were built on knowledge alone, we'd see a lot more of them. But information doesn't create transformation. I'll be honest with you: I'm not a fan of leadership and teambuilding book clubs, not because I don't believe in reading. I read about thirty books a year across different disciplines to find insights and ways to improve my skills and effectiveness. I don't like book clubs because, too often, leaders get fooled into thinking they've done the work simply because they can sit around and recite concepts from a book. They discuss the ideas, maybe even debate the nuances, but then fail to do what it takes to implement what they've learned long enough to actually make the concepts viable. The meeting becomes the deliverable rather than the starting point.

Most teams stay average or struggle, not because they don't care, and not because they don't understand what needs to change. They stay stuck because they don't follow through consistently enough to make new practices viable.

The research is clear: According to Harvard Business School, seventy percent of strategic initiatives fail not because of poor strategy, but because of poor execution. The same principle applies to team development. The gap isn't in understanding; it's in implementation.

The gap isn't in understanding; it's in implementation.

That's why this master blueprint began with an initial chapter designed as a soil test, ensuring that the great team you're about to build has a foundation of bedrock. That bedrock is found in the leader who says, "I believe the work involved in building a great team is worth the investment it's going to take." Reading this book and nodding along means nothing. What matters is whether you'll do the uncomfortable work of actually applying these principles tomorrow, next week, and six months from now when the novelty has worn off and the real discipline begins.

Expect Resistance: Lead Anyway

Change always meets resistance, and that's actually a good sign. It means you're doing something that matters.

You'll hear things like, "This is how we've always done it," or "That sounds good in theory, but it won't work here." Some people will push back, testing whether you're serious about this change. Others will watch from the sidelines, waiting to see if this is just another passing initiative. And you might even catch yourself falling back into old patterns when stress hits or motivation fades.

None of that means you've failed. It just means you're doing the real work.

Here's what I've learned personally and from working with hundreds of teams: Resistance isn't a barrier to change, it's part of the process. The leaders, coaches, parents, and partners who successfully transform their environments don't avoid resistance. They expect it, prepare for it, and lead through it.

The resistance will come in predictable forms:

From others: "We don't have time for this," "Our situation is different," or the silent compliance that never turns into genuine engagement.

From yourself: The temptation to revert to old habits under pressure, the doubt that creeps in when progress feels slow, the overwhelming urge to fix everything at once instead of staying focused.

But here's what separates those who succeed from those who give up: They understand that resistance is temporary, but the impact of consistent behavior is permanent.

Great teams aren't built overnight. But they are built—one consistent behavior at a time, one conversation at a time, one small act of support, celebration, or challenge at a time. So expect resistance. Plan for it. And then keep going anyway. Because the alternative of staying where you are isn't really an alternative at all. Not when you know what's possible.

> Great teams aren't built overnight. But they are built— one consistent behavior at a time.

Your Personal Action Plan: The Foundation

Before diving into role-specific strategies, every leader, coach, parent, and partner needs to start with the same foundation.

STEP 1: TAKE INVENTORY

Before you can improve your team, you need to see it clearly. Ask yourself:

- Are we truly supporting each other, or is it every person for themself?
- Do we celebrate progress, or only focus on what went wrong?
- Are we challenging each other in ways that build growth, or just applying pressure?
- Are we living out the CABLES Behaviors daily?
- Are our team's core needs being met?

Be honest. This isn't about judgment; it's about clarity.

STEP 2: CHOOSE ONE FOCUS AREA

Don't try to change everything at once. You do not need to boil the ocean. Pick one behavior to improve:

- Low trust? Start with Consistency.
- Low engagement? Start with Appreciation.
- Poor communication? Start with Authentic Listening.
- Low motivation? Focus on Empowerment.

Master one, then build from there.

STEP 3: START THE CONVERSATION

Culture change isn't a solo act. Ask your team:

- What makes us a great team when we're at our best?
- What gets in our way?
- What's one thing we could do differently together?

You don't have to fix everything in one meeting. Just start.
People support what they help create.

STEP 4: MEASURE, ADJUST, REPEAT

Reinforce progress. Celebrate small wins. Adjust what isn't working.
Pay attention to which direction your one percent change is going.
Keep asking:

- What's improving?
- What still needs attention?
- How are we growing?

For distributed teams, add these measurement approaches:

- Schedule regular virtual check-ins specifically focused on culture and behavior change.
- Use collaboration tools to track progress on CABLES Behaviors across the team.
- Create digital systems for peer feedback and recognition.
- Establish clear metrics for virtual engagement and connection.

Sustainable change is a cycle, not a switch.

Role-Specific Implementation Strategies

Now that you have the foundation, here's how to tailor your approach based on your specific context:

FOR LEADERS: BUILDING TEAM CULTURE

PHASE 1 (WEEKS 1–4): FOUNDATION SETTING

Building on your personal action plan:
Take Inventory: Leadership Style:

- Assess your team using the CABLES framework: Which behaviors are you modeling consistently?
- Use the NEEDS Model to identify which needs aren't being met.
- Survey team members (formally or informally) about current culture.

Choose Focus + Leadership Application:

- If trust is low: Focus on Consistency in your communications, decisions, and follow-through.
- If engagement is low: Start with daily Appreciation practices.
- If communication is poor: Commit to Authentic Listening in every one-on-one.
- If motivation is low: Focus on Empowerment by involving team in decisions.

Start Conversation: Team Level:

- Hold team meeting using the three questions from step 3.
- Share the Support-Celebrate-Challenge framework.
- Ask: "Which of these three do we do well? Which needs attention?"
- Invite team input on implementation approach.
- Talk about ownership over accountability.

Measure/Adjust: Leadership Metrics:

- Weekly team-pulse checks on engagement and support.
- Track your consistency in chosen CABLES Behavior.

- Monitor team participation and energy levels.
- Adjust approach based on team feedback.

PHASE 2 (WEEKS 5–12): HABIT BUILDING

- Implement weekly recognition practices (celebrate wins, acknowledge effort).
- Use the CATCH Model for performance conversations.
- Create team rituals that reinforce belonging.
- Apply the SET framework to team goals.

PHASE 3 (WEEKS 13+): CULTURE INTEGRATION

- Train other leaders in the framework.
- Make Support-Celebrate-Challenge part of performance reviews.
- Expand successful practices across the organization.
- Mentor others in implementation.

FOR COACHES: DEVELOPING ATHLETES AND TEAMS

PHASE 1 (WEEKS 1–4): RELATIONSHIP BUILDING

Building on your personal action plan:

Take Inventory: Coaching Style:

- Assess team dynamics: Do players support each other or compete internally?
- Evaluate your celebration practices: Do you only recognize performance or also character/effort?
- Review your challenge approach: Is it building resilience or creating fear?

Choose Focus + Coaching Application:

- Low trust: Focus on Consistency in your expectations and responses.
- Low team cohesion: Start with Belongingness practices.
- Poor communication: Commit to Authentic Listening with each athlete.

- Low motivation: Focus on Empowerment by involving players in team decisions.

Start Conversation: Team Level:

- Team meeting: "What makes us strongest as a team?"
- Individual conversations: Use the framework to understand each player's needs.
- Ask: "How can I better support, celebrate, and challenge you?"

Measure/Adjust: Coaching Metrics:

- Weekly assessment of team chemistry and individual engagement.
- Track your consistency in a chosen behavior.
- Monitor player feedback and team-performance trends.

PHASE 2 (WEEKS 5–12): MOMENTUM CREATION

- Implement consistent celebration of effort, improvement, and character.
- Use Empathy when addressing setbacks or poor performance.
- Apply the Challenge pillar gradually, building on established trust.
- Help players set individual goals using the SET framework.

PHASE 3 (WEEKS 13+): SUSTAINED EXCELLENCE

- Create player leadership opportunities.
- Establish team-accountability systems.
- Model teammate behaviors you want to see.

FOR PARENTS: STRENGTHENING FAMILY BONDS

PHASE 1 (WEEKS 1–4): CONNECTION BUILDING

Building on your personal action plan:

Take Inventory: Family Style:

- Assess family dynamics: Do family members support each other during challenges?

- Evaluate recognition patterns: Do you celebrate character and effort or just achievements?
- Review your challenge approach: Are you building resilience or just enforcing rules?

Choose Focus + Parenting Application:

- Low connection: Focus on Belongingness through family rituals and one-on-one time.
- Low confidence in children: Start with daily Appreciation for character traits.
- Poor family communication: Commit to Authentic Listening during daily interactions.
- Low motivation in children: Focus on Empowerment by involving kids in family decisions.

Start Conversation: Family Level:

- Family meeting: "What makes our family special? What could make it even better?"
- Have individual conversations with each child about their needs and interests.
- Ask your spouse/partner: "How can we better support, celebrate, and challenge our kids together?"

Measure/Adjust: Family Metrics:

- Weekly family mood and connection assessment.
- Track consistency in a chosen behavior.
- Monitor children's engagement and behavior patterns.

PHASE 2 (WEEKS 5–12): STRUCTURE AND GROWTH

- Establish family rituals that reinforce support and celebration.
- Use age-appropriate challenges that build responsibility.
- Apply SET to family goals (chores, screen time, activities).
- Create systems for family members to support each other.

PHASE 3 (WEEKS 13+): LONG-TERM DEVELOPMENT

- Teach children to support, celebrate, and challenge siblings.
- Model behaviors you want them to carry into their own relationships.
- Adjust your approach as children grow while maintaining core principles.

FOR PARTNERS: DEEPENING RELATIONSHIPS

Phase 1 (Weeks 1–4): Rebuilding Foundation

Building on your personal action plan:

Take Inventory: Relationship Style:

- Assess relationship dynamics: Do you truly support each other's goals and challenges?
- Evaluate appreciation patterns: Do you celebrate daily contributions or take them for granted?
- Review conflict approach: Are disagreements helping you grow or creating distance?

Choose Focus + Relationship Application:

- Low trust: Focus on Consistency between words and actions.
- Feeling unappreciated: Start with daily Appreciation for contributions and character.
- Poor communication: Commit to Authentic Listening during conversations.
- Feeling stuck: Focus on Empowerment by supporting each other's individual goals.

Start Conversation: Partnership Level:

- Relationship check-in: "When do we feel most connected? What gets in our way?"
- Individual reflection: "How can I better support, celebrate, and challenge my partner?"
- Ask: "What would make you feel most supported/appreciated/ challenged to grow?"

Measure/Adjust: Relationship Metrics:

- Weekly relationship satisfaction and connection assessment.
- Track consistency in a chosen behavior.
- Monitor communication patterns and conflict resolution.

PHASE 2 (WEEKS 5–12): STRENGTHENING CONNECTION

- Create regular celebration of relationship wins and personal growth.
- Apply constructive challenge using CATCH Model for difficult conversations.
- Set shared goals using SET framework.
- Establish rituals that reinforce support and appreciation.

PHASE 3 (WEEKS 13+): THRIVING TOGETHER

- Support each other's individual growth and goals.
- Celebrate your relationship's resilience and strength.
- Challenge each other to grow while maintaining deep connection.
- Model healthy relationship behaviors for others.

Universal Implementation Principles

Regardless of your role, these principles apply to successful implementation:

START SMALL, BUILD CONSISTENTLY

- Choose one CABLES Behavior to focus on initially.
- Practice it daily until it becomes natural.
- Add additional behaviors only after the first is established.

EXPECT THE IMPLEMENTATION DIP

- Weeks 3–6 are typically the hardest.
- Motivation will fade: rely on systems and habits.
- Small setbacks don't mean failure, they mean you're human.

INVOLVE OTHERS IN THE PROCESS

- Share the framework with your team/family/partner.
- Ask for feedback on your implementation.
- Celebrate progress together.
- Adjust your approach based on their input.

FOCUS ON PROCESS OVER OUTCOMES

- Measure your consistency in applying behaviors.
- Track engagement and connection, not just results.
- Celebrate effort and improvement.

Stay patient with the timeline for culture change.

Virtual-Team Implementation Considerations

Hybrid and remote teams require modified approaches to ensure successful implementation:

Creating Virtual Accountability: Assign implementation partners who check in with each other regularly via video calls or messaging. What used to happen through casual office interactions must now be scheduled and intentional.

Digital Recognition Systems: Use collaboration platforms to create visible appreciation channels where team members can celebrate each other's progress in real time. Make recognition public and permanent rather than fleeting.

Structured Virtual Touchpoints: Schedule regular "culture check-ins" during team meetings where people can share implementation successes and challenges. This creates the group support that drives sustained change.

Hybrid Inclusion Strategies: Ensure remote team members receive equal attention and support during implementation. Use rotation systems to guarantee virtual participants get recognition and accountability support.

Technology as an Enabler: Leverage digital tools to track consistency in CABLES Behaviors, send reminder notifications, and create shared visibility into team-culture progress.

The key insight is that virtual implementation requires more structure and intentionality, but can be just as effective as in-person approaches when properly designed.

Your Legacy Begins Now

At the end of the day, people won't remember you for how many meetings you ran or how many tasks you checked off. They'll remember how you made them feel. Did you make them feel supported? Seen? Valued? Did you challenge them in a way that helped them grow?

That's what great teammates do. That's what great leaders do.

You now have more than just the roadmap: you have the blueprint. You have the NEEDS Model to understand what drives people. You have the CABLES Behaviors to build strong relationships. You have the framework of Support, Celebrate, and Challenge to guide daily actions. You have SET to turn intentions into achievements.

But tools are only as powerful as the commitment to use them.

The teams and leaders who transform cultures don't do so because they have perfect conditions or unlimited resources. They succeed because they decide to start where they are, with what they have, for the people they serve.

Your influence doesn't require a title. It doesn't require permission. It requires choice—the choice to show up differently, to model the behaviors you want to see, to persist when others might quit.

The bridge between where your team is and where it could be? You're building it. Every consistent action. Every moment of authentic listening. Every celebration of progress. Every constructive challenge. You're laying the foundation for something that will outlast your tenure and impact people you may never fully know you've influenced.

That's not just leadership. That's legacy.

The Final Challenge

I want to leave you with one final challenge: not because you need more pressure, but because you deserve to see what you're truly capable of.

For the next thirty days, commit to one specific behavior from this book. Not three. Not five. One.

Maybe it's:

- Starting every team meeting by recognizing one person's contribution.
- Having one authentic-listening conversation each day.
- Using the CATCH Model the next time you need to address a performance issue.
- Setting one SET goal for your own leadership development.
- Implementing one family ritual that builds connection.

For virtual teams, consider implementation approaches like:

- Creating shared digital accountability tracking.
- Scheduling weekly virtual coffee chats focused on culture building.
- Using video messages for recognition and feedback.
- Establishing online peer-mentoring relationships.

Whatever you choose, do it for thirty days. Track your consistency. Notice what changes—in yourself, in others, in the environment around you.

Then, if you're willing, share your story. Email me at *patrick@ emeryleadershipgroup.com*. Tell me what you tried, what worked, what didn't, and what you learned. Your experience might become the encouragement someone else needs to take their first step.

The world needs more great teams. More great teammates. More people who understand that excellence isn't just about performance: it's about how we treat each other in the pursuit of something meaningful.

You have everything you need. The only question left is: What are you going to build?

ACKNOWLEDGEMENTS

My deepest gratitude goes to **my wife, Cyndi, and our children, Josh, Grace, and Noah**. You are the most important and greatest team I will ever be part of. Your love, patience, and support are the foundation for everything I teach and strive to live. You remind me every day what great teams truly look like.

I also want to extend my sincere appreciation to those who graciously offered their time, insight, and honest feedback as early readers of this manuscript. Your thoughtful perspectives helped refine and strengthen this work in meaningful ways.

Stuart Glass, Christi Green, Jude Killey, Dru Khaira, Peter Madigan, Andy Pettola, Liv Skerry, and Mike Stelmach Thank you for your invaluable contributions. Your encouragement and candid feedback made this a stronger and more complete blueprint to build a great team.

A special thank you to **Stuart Glass** and **Liv Skerry**, who have been instrumental in helping me implement and refine this model as we introduced it to several hundred of their managers and teams. Their dedication to developing others and leading through example demonstrates what it truly means to build great teams.

WORKS CITED

INTRODUCTION: DON'T HOPE FOR A GREAT TEAM—BUILD ONE

Duckworth, A. *Grit: The Power of Passion and Perseverance.* Scribner, 2016.

Dweck, C.S. *Mindset: The New Psychology of Success.* Random House, 2006.

Edmonson, A.C. *The Fearless Organization: Creating Psychological Safety in the Workplace for Learning, Innovation, and Growth.* John Wiley & Sons, 2018.

Ryan, R.M. and Deci, E.L. *Self-Determination Theory: Basic Psychological Needs in Motivation, Development, and Wellness.* Guilford Press, 2017.

CHAPTER 1: GREAT TEAMS AND ONE PERCENT

Duckworth, A. *Grit: The Power of Passion and Perseverance.* Scribner, 2016.

Dweck, C.S. *Mindset: The New Psychology of Success.* Random House, 2006.

Edmonson, A.C. *The Fearless Organization: Creating Psychological Safety in the Workplace for Learning, Innovation, and Growth.* John Wiley & Sons, 2018.

Gottman, J.M. and Silver, N. *The Seven Principles for Making Marriage Work: A Practical Guide from the Country's Foremost Relationship Expert.* Harmony Books, 2015.

Zak, P. J. *The Moral Molecule: The Source of Love and Prosperity.* Dutton, 2012. Chapter 2: The power of a "believe' System

CHAPTER 2: THE POWER OF A "BELIEVE" SYSTEM

The Arbinger Institute, *Leadership and Self-Deception: Getting out of the box.* Berrett-Koehler Publishers, 2010.

Dweck, C.S. *Mindset: The New Psychology of Success.* Random House, 2006.

CHAPTER 3: THE NEEDS MODEL: A FOUNDATION FOR STRONGER TEAMS, FAMILIES, AND RELATIONSHIPS

Edmonson, A.C. *The Fearless Organization: Creating Psychological Safety in the Workplace for Learning, Innovation, and Growth.* John Wiley & Sons, 2018.

Gottman, J. M. *The Relationship Cure: A 5 Step Guide to Strengthening Your Marriage, Family, and Friendships.* Harmony Books, 2001.

Maslow, A.H. "A Theory of Human Motivation." *Psychological Review* 50, no. 4 (1943): 370-396.

Ryan, R.M. and Deci, E.L. "Self-Determination Theory and the Facilitation of Intrinsic Motivation, Social Development, and Well-Being." *American Psychologist* 55, no. 1 (2000): 68-78.

CHAPTER 4:
BUILDING THE BRIDGES THAT CARRY TEAMS TO SUCCESS

Schafer, J., and Karlins, M. *The Like Switch: An Ex-FBI Agent's Guide to Influencing, Attracting, and Winning People Over.* Touchstone, 2015.

Sullivan, D., and Hardy, B. *The Gap and the Gain: The High Achiever's Guide to Happiness, Confidence, and Success.* Hay House Inc., 2021.

Veroneau, P., *The Leadership Bridge,* 2022.

CHAPTER 5:
GREAT TEAMS CAN ONLY EXIST WITH GREATE TEAMMATES

Emmons, R. A., and McCullough, M.E. "Counting Blessings Versus Burdens: An Experimental Investigation of Gratitude and Subjective Well-Being in Daily Life." *Journal of Personality and Social Psychology* 84, no. 2 (2003): 377-389.

Farnsworth, W. *The Practicing Stoic: A Philosopher User's Manual.* David R. Godine, 2018.

Moawad, T., and Staples, A. *It Takes What It Takes: How to Think Neutrally and Gain Control of Your Life.* HarperOne, 2020.

Sullivan, D., and Hardy, B. *The Gap and The Gain: The High Achiever's Guide to Happiness, Confidence, and Success.* Hay House, 2021.

CHAPTER 6: ARE YOU SET FOR SUCCESS?

Coyle, D. *The Talent Code: Greatness Isn't Born. It's Grown. Here's How.* Bantam Books, 2009.

Duckworth, A. *Grit: The Power of Passion and Perseverance.* Scribner, 2016.

Locke., E. A., and Lantham, G.P. "Building a Practically Useful Theory of Goal Setting and Task Motivation: A 35-Year Odyssey." *American Psychologist* 57, no. 9 (2002) 705-717.

Ryan, R.M., and Deci, E.L. *Self-Determination Theory: Basic Psychological Needs in Motivation, Development, and Wellness.* Guilford Press, 2017.

CHAPTER 7: WHY SUPPORT COMES FIRST

Keteylan, A., and Talty, J. *The Price: What It Takes to Win in College Football's Era of Chaos.* Twelve, 2022.

Waldinger, R., and Schulz, M. *The Good Life: Lessons from the World's Longest Scientific Study of Happiness.* Simon & Schuster, 2023.

CHAPTER 8: WHY CELEBRATION MATTERS

Amabile, T., and Kramer, S. *The Progress Principle: Using Small Wins to Ignite Joy, Engagement, and Creativity at Work.* Harvard Business Review Press, 2011.

Gallup, Inc., Employee Engagement Survey.

CHAPTER 9: WHY CHALLENGE COMES LAST

(No formal publications were cited in this chapter; the content relies on illustrative examples and the author's CATCH Model.)

CHAPTER 10:
TURNING INSIGHT INTO ACTION: OWNERSHIP UNCOVERED

Beer, M., and Nohria,N. "Cracking the Code of Change." *Harvard Business Review* 78, no. 3 (2000): 133-141.

ABOUT THE AUTHOR

Patrick Veroneau is the CEO and founder of **Emery Leadership Group**. He has dedicated his career to helping individuals, teams, and organizations become great. For more than two decades, Patrick has worked with leaders and teams in manufacturing, construction, healthcare, higher education, and athletics. His message is clear: Greatness is not reserved for a few, it is built through consistent behaviors practiced by everyone.

A consultant, speaker, coach, and bestselling author, Patrick is known for turning complex research into clear, practical frameworks that help people change how they lead and connect. His evidence-based models, including **CABLES**, **NEEDS**, **SET GOALS**, and **CATCH**, are used by Fortune 500 companies, Division I athletic programs, and small businesses to build trust, strengthen engagement, and inspire ownership.

Patrick is the author of *The Leadership Bridge: How to Engage Your Employees and Drive Organizational Excellence* and *The Missing Piece: What Great Teams Do That Others Overlook*. In his work, he challenges traditional views of accountability and shows that true greatness comes from ownership, a mindset that transforms compliance into commitment and performance into purpose.

In addition to his books and consulting, Patrick hosts the **Learning from Leaders Podcast**, where he interviews influential thinkers and high performers to uncover the behaviors that separate average teams from extraordinary ones. His workshops and keynotes combine practical insight with authentic storytelling, helping people become not just better leaders but better teammates and contributors in every area of their lives. Patrick lives in Maine with his wife, Cyndi, and their three children, Grace, Josh, and Noah. He often says they are the greatest team he has ever been a part of. To learn more about Patrick, his work, and upcoming programs, visit www.emeryleadershipgroup.com or connect with him on LinkedIn using the QR Code below.

EMERY LEADERSHIP GROUP

Emery Leadership Group and Patrick Veroneau are helping individuals and organizations become great through personal transformation and a powerful shift from chasing accountability to creating ownership.

Consulting: Emery Leadership Group partners with organizations to build great individuals and teams through practical, research-based workshops on leadership, communication, and trust. Each program is customized to strengthen ownership and collaboration at every level.

Speaking: Patrick Veroneau inspires audiences with engaging stories and approaches that bring his proven frameworks to life. His keynotes connect research, real stories, and practical action in a way that challenges teams to rise above their best and become great.

Customized Programs & Resources:

The Missing Piece and CABLE Leadership online courses and digital tools were created to help leaders and teammates apply these concepts daily. Participants gain the mindset, models, and methods needed to create teams that don't just perform—they thrive.

Email Patrick at Patrick@emeryleadershipgroup.com or schedule an exploratory meeting to learn more with the QR code below.

BOOK PATRICK VERONEAU, MS
TO SPEAK WITH YOUR TEAM, PROGRAM, OR ORGANIZATION

Patrick is represented by The Gray + Miller Agency, a leading speaking bureau representing some of the world's most engaging and influential speakers, authors, and thought leaders.

For speaking inquiries please visit **graymilleragency.com**

or submit a request at **info@emeryleadershipgroup.com**

Representing a community of authors whose books have collectively sold hundreds of millions of copies, the founders of The Gray + Miller Agency launched Maison Vero, a professional publishing house that partners with rising authors to bring their thought leadership to the world. Our representation covers every aspect of thought leadership including U.S. senators, governors, and ambassadors, billionaire founders and entrepreneurs, researchers, academics, scientists, consultants practitioners, social influencers, C-suite leaders, adventurers professional athletes, artists, and creators. We partner with thought leaders and world changers like you who have a story to tell. By bringing decades of professional expertise to our clients, we are charting a new path in a timeless industry that transcends publishing norms transforming powerful thoughts into impactful books that inspire minds ignite hearts, and open doors.

Visit maisonvero.com to view our growing list of authors, or to submit a proposal for publication consideration.

Follow Maison Vero for insight and inspiration on social media:

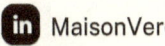 MaisonVero   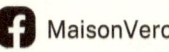 MaisonVero   MaisonVeroPublishing

For information about special discounts for bulk purchases, please call 1-949-333-4872 or email info@graymilleragency.com.

Maison Vero is a partner brand of The Gray + Miller Agency, a speaking, literary and talent consortium. For more information on the talent represented by The Gray + Miller Agency, or to bring any of our thought leaders to your organization or live event, please visit our website at graymilleragency.com.

www.ingramcontent.com/pod-product-compliance
Lightning Source LLC
Chambersburg PA
CBHW021147130626
46554CB00005B/1698